William Shakespeare's
HENRY IV,
PART ONE

NOTES

A CONTEMPORARY
LITERARY VIEWS BOOK

Edited and with an Introduction by
HAROLD BLOOM

First Printing
1 3 5 7 9 8 6 4 2

Cover Illustration: - Peasants Playing Cards in a Tavern, Adriaen Brouwer; Alte Pinakothek Museum, Munich Bayerisches Nationalmuseum

Library of Congress Cataloging-in-Publication Data

William Shakespeare's Henry IV, part 1 / edited and with an introduction by Harold Bloom.
p. cm. – (Bloom's notes)
Includes bibliographical references and index.
Summary: Includes a brief biography of the author, thematic and structural analysis of the work, critical views, and an index of themes and ideas.
ISBN 0-7910-4060-7
1. Shakespeare, William, 1564–1616. King Henry IV. Part 1. 2. Henry IV, King of England, 1367–1413—In literature. [1. Shakespeare, William, 1564–1616. King Henry IV. Part 1. 2. English literature—History and criticism.] I. Bloom, Harold. II. Series.
PR2810.W5 1995
822.3'3—dc20
95-43499
CIP
AC

Chelsea House Publishers
1974 Sproul Road, Suite 400
P.O. Box 914
Broomall, PA 19008-0914

Contents

User's Guide

This volume is designed to present biographical, critical, and bibliographical information on William Shakespeare and *Henry IV, Part One*. Following Harold Bloom's introduction, there appears a detailed biography of the author, discussing the major events in his life and his important literary works. Then follows a thematic and structural analysis of the work, in which significant themes, patterns, and motifs are traced. An annotated list of characters supplies brief information on the chief characters in the work.

A selection of critical extracts, derived from previously published material by leading critics, then follows. The extracts consist of such things as statements by the author on his work, early notices of the work, and later evaluations down to the present day. The items are arranged chronologically by date of first publication. A bibliography of Shakespeare's writings (including a complete listing of all books he wrote, cowrote, edited, and translated, and selected posthumous publications), a list of additional books and articles on him and on *Henry IV, Part One,* and an index of themes and ideas conclude the volume.

Harold Bloom is Sterling Professor of the Humanities at Yale University and Henry W. and Albert A. Berg Professor of English at the New York University Graduate School. He is the author of twenty books and the editor of more than thirty anthologies of literature and literary criticism.

Professor Bloom's works include *Shelley's Mythmaking* (1959), *The Visionary Company* (1961), *Blake's Apocalypse* (1963), *Yeats* (1970), *A Map of Misreading* (1975), *Kabbalah and Criticism* (1975), and *Agon: Towards a Theory of Revisionism* (1982). *The Anxiety of Influence* (1973) sets forth Professor Bloom's provocative theory of the literary relationships between the great writers and their predecessors. His most recent books are *The American Religion* (1992) and *The Western Canon* (1994).

Professor Bloom earned his Ph.D. from Yale University in 1955 and has served on the Yale faculty since then. He is a 1985 MacArthur Foundation Award recipient and served as the Charles Eliot Norton Professor of Poetry at Harvard University in 1987–88. He is currently the editor of the Chelsea House series Major Literary Characters and Modern Critical Views, and other Chelsea House series in literary criticism.

Introduction

HAROLD BLOOM

In the four centuries since *Henry IV, Part One* (1597) first was played, the audiences and readers of all nations have rejoiced to agree with Shakespeare's original playgoers that Sir John Falstaff is their universal favorite among all his characters, except perhaps for Hamlet. The only dissenters have been academic moralists, including many modern scholars of Shakespeare, who persist in the curious enterprise of bestowing their moral disapproval upon the greatest comic hero (or hero-villain, if you prefer) in all of Western literature. The Falstaff of the two *Henry IV* plays must not be confused with the Falstaff of *The Merry Wives of Windsor,* who became the Falstaff of Verdi's grand opera. Shakespeare's true Falstaff is no mere roisterer or Lord of Misrule. Rather, he is the veritable brother of Don Quixote and Sancho Panza in Cervantes's great book, and also is near allied to the extraordinary Panurge of Rabelais. Falstaff shares in both the Don's and Sancho's varieties of wisdom, and he has something close to the heroic vitality of Panurge. Even closer than all these is a likely actual influence upon Shakespeare's creation of Falstaff, Chaucer's the Wife of Bath in *The Canterbury Tales.* The Wife of Bath proclaims that she has had her world as in her time, an assertion Falstaff need not bother to make, because for him it would be redundant. In *Henry IV, Part One,* Falstaff is triumphant over the state and over all the forces aligned against him, even over time itself. Sir John nimbly steps aside, and bids the world of "honor" pass, and it does. Secure in himself as the monarch of wit, he needs no other kingdom.

It might be useful to list all the things Sir John Falstaff is *not,* if only because so many scholars have indicted him for all of these sins, faults, crimes, and flaws. He is not: a coward, a politician, an opportunist, a fool or court jester, a whoremonger, an alcoholic, a seducer of youth. Unlike his detractors, he is also not a bore, or a hypocrite, or a sanctimonious puritan. Lord of language, Falstaff is so vast an intelligence that we apprehend his mind to be greater even in girth than is his body. Almost everything he says in the two *Henry IV* plays needs pondering and will reward the reader all the more the longer such consideration continues. Hamlet undoubtedly is the only character in all of Western literature who displays an authorial consciousness of his own, but Hamlet has faith neither in language nor in himself. Falstaff has identified himself with language and has made language entirely his own. Faith or faithlessness, whether in language or the self, is irrelevant to him. No other literary character possesses or emanates such delight in language. It is largely because of Falstaff that we must judge Shakespeare to have written not only the best poetry we have ever read, but also the best prose.

Falstaff, for all his epiphanies of wit, has darker elements in him, just as his rival, Hamlet, is deeply infested by the destructive principle. Though not perhaps as old as King Lear, Falstaff is of immense age, and his courageous defiance of time has an undersong of great pathos, particularly in someone whose motto is: "Give me life." A veteran warrior of considerable reputation, Falstaff has pierced through the mask of military reputation, with its childish exaltations of honor and glory, and has found the skull smirking beneath: "I like not such grinning honor as Sir Walter hath." Shakespeare's largest tribute to Falstaff comes in his deliberate exclusion of the fat knight from *Henry V,* a play that Sir John would have destroyed merely by his living presence. Not even a dying Falstaff is risked by Shakespeare; we receive only the immense art of Mistress Quickly's touching account of the great wit's deathbed scene. What chance would the patriotic rant of King Henry V have against the sublime mockery of Falstaff's irreverence? There is a sly implication throughout the play that Falstaff's old pupil, Prince Hal, does not always believe everything that King Henry V says, but consider how difficult it would be for the former Prince Hal to say anything at all about battle's "happy few," if Falstaff were anywhere nearby on the stage.

Like so many Shakespearean plays, *Henry IV, Part One* has a long foreground that we must put together for ourselves if we are to grasp the opening scenes of the drama. Every early scene between Hal and Falstaff is one of thrust and parry, with the prince obsessively, almost murderously, on the offensive.

An initial, profound attachment to Falstaff, really a student-teacher relationship, evidently has been long replaced by a growing ambivalence towards Sir John on Hal's part. As the play proceeds, the ambivalence discards its positive affect, and the prince stalks Falstaff, anxious to convict the comic hero of cowardice, and particularly eager to compel Sir John to admit it. Hal comes very close to handing Falstaff over to the hangman and shows something less than a mountain of grief when he is deceived by the brilliant feigner into the notion that Sir John has been slain by Douglas, the "hot termagant Scot." Who is the counterfeit: Falstaff who feigns death so as to become "the true and perfect image of life," or the wily Hal, who boasts despicably that he has been slumming with Falstaff so that his reformed self will shine more brightly for his future subjects? When Falstaff says to Hal, "I am not a double man," we have to reflect that Hal most certainly is one. Whatever scholarship goes on doing to Falstaff, Sir John sublimely will bury all of his undertakers. He changed Shakespeare's art permanently. After Falstaff, the great Shakespearean characters come crowding upon us, for the largest of comic geniuses seems to have taught Shakespeare himself that there were no limits to his art. ✤

Biography of William Shakespeare

Few events in the life of William Shakespeare are supported by reliable evidence, and many incidents recorded by commentators of the last four centuries are either conjectural or apocryphal.

William Shakespeare was born in Stratford-upon-Avon on April 22 or 23, 1564, the son of Mary Arden and John Shakespeare, a tradesman. His very early education was in the hands of a tutor, for his parents were probably illiterate. At age seven he entered the Free School in Stratford, where he learned the "small Latin and less Greek" attributed to him by Ben Jonson. When not in school Shakespeare may have gone to the popular Stratford fairs and to the dramas and mystery plays performed by traveling actors.

When Shakespeare was about thirteen his father removed him from school and apprenticed him to a butcher, although it is not known how long he remained in this occupation. When he was eighteen he married Anne Hathaway; their first child, Susanna, was born six months later. A pair of twins, Hamnet and Judith, were born in February 1585. About this time Shakespeare was caught poaching deer on the estate of Sir Thomas Lucy of Charlecot; Lucy's prosecution is said to have inspired Shakespeare to write his earliest literary work, a satire on his opponent. Shakespeare was convicted of poaching and forced to leave Stratford. He withdrew to London, leaving his family behind. He soon attached himself to the stage, initially in a menial capacity (as tender of playgoers' horses, according to one tradition), then as a prompter's attendant. When the poaching furor subsided, Shakespeare returned to Stratford to join one of the many bands of itinerant actors. In the next five years he gained what little theatre training he received.

By 1592 Shakespeare was a recognized actor, and in that year he wrote and produced his first play, *Henry VI, Part One.* Its success impelled Shakespeare soon afterward to write the second and third parts of *Henry VI.* (Many early and modern critics believed that *Love's Labour's Lost* preceded these histories as Shakespeare's earliest play, but the majority of modern scholars discount this theory.) Shakespeare's popularity provoked the jealousy of Robert Greene, as recorded in his posthumous *Groats-worth of Wit* (1592).

In 1593 Shakespeare published *Venus and Adonis,* a long poem based upon Ovid (or perhaps upon Arthur Golding's translation of Ovid's *Metamorphoses*). It was dedicated to the young earl of Southampton—but perhaps without permission, a possible indication that Shakespeare was trying to gain the nobleman's patronage. However, the dedicatory address to Southampton in the poem *The Rape of Lucrece* (1594) reveals Shakespeare to have been on good terms with him. Many plays—such as *Titus Andronicus, The Comedy of Errors,* and *Romeo and Juliet*—were produced over the next several years, most performed by Shakespeare's troupe, the Lord Chamberlain's Company. In December 1594 Shakespeare acted in a comedy (of unknown authorship) before Queen Elizabeth; many other royal performances followed in the next decade.

In August 1596 Shakespeare's son Hamnet died. Early the next year Shakespeare bought a home, New Place, in the center of Stratford; he is said to have planted a mulberry tree in the backyard with his own hands. Shakespeare's relative prosperity is indicated by his purchasing more than a hundred acres of farmland in 1602, a cottage near his estate later that year, and half-interest in the tithes of some local villages in 1605.

In September 1598 Shakespeare began his friendship with the then unknown Ben Jonson by producing his play *Every Man in His Humour.* The next year the publisher William Jaggard affixed Shakespeare's name, without his permission, to a curious medley of poems under the title *The Passionate Pilgrim;* the majority of the poems were not by Shakespeare. Two of his sonnets, however, appeared in this collection, although the 154 sonnets, with their mysterious dedication to "Mr. W. H.," were not published as a group until 1609. Also in 1599 the Globe Theatre was built in Southwark (an area of London), and Shakespeare's company began acting there. Many of his greatest plays—*Troilus and Cressida, King Lear, Othello, Macbeth*—

were performed in the Globe before its destruction by fire in 1613.

The death in 1603 of Queen Elizabeth, the last of the Tudors, and the accession of James I, from the Stuart dynasty of Scotland, created anxiety throughout England. Shakespeare's fortunes, however, were unaffected, as the new monarch extended the license of Shakespeare's company to perform at the Globe. James I saw a performance of *Othello* at the court in November 1604. In October 1605 Shakespeare's company performed before the Mayor and Corporation of Oxford.

The last five years of Shakespeare's life seem void of incident; he had retired from the stage by 1613. Among the few known incidents is Shakespeare's involvement in a heated and lengthy dispute about the enclosure of common-fields around Stratford. He died on April 23, 1616, and was buried in the Church of St. Mary's in Stratford. A monument was later erected to him in the Poets' Corner of Westminster Abbey.

Numerous corrupt quarto editions of Shakespeare's plays were published during his lifetime. These editions, based either on manuscripts, promptbooks, or sometimes merely actors' recollections of the plays, were meant to capitalize on Shakespeare's renown. Other plays, now deemed wholly or largely spurious—*Edward III, The Yorkshire Tragedy, The Two Noble Kinsmen,* and others—were also published under Shakespeare's name during and after his lifetime. Shakespeare's plays were collected in the First Folio of 1623 by John Heminge and Henry Condell. Nine years later the Second Folio was published, and in 1640 Shakespeare's poems were collected. The first standard collected edition was by Nicholas Rowe (1709), followed by the editions of Alexander Pope (1725), Lewis Theobald (1733), Samuel Johnson (1765), Edmond Malone (1790), and many others.

Shakespeare's plays are now customarily divided into the following categories (probable dates of writing are given in brackets): comedies (*The Comedy of Errors* [1590], *The Taming of the Shrew* [1592], *The Two Gentlemen of Verona* [1592–93], *A Midsummer Night's Dream* [1595], *Love's Labour's Lost* [1595], *The Merchant of Venice* [1596–98], *As You Like It*

[1597], *The Merry Wives of Windsor* [1597], *Much Ado About Nothing* [1598–99], *Twelfth Night* [1601], *All's Well That Ends Well* [1603–04], and *Measure for Measure* [1604]); histories (*Henry VI, Part One* [1590–92], *Henry VI, Parts Two and Three* [1590–92], *Richard III* [1591], *King John* [1591–98], *Richard II* [1595], *Henry IV, Part One* [1597], *Henry IV, Part Two* [1597], *Henry V* [1599], and *Henry VIII* [1613]); tragedies (*Titus Andronicus* [1590], *Romeo and Juliet* [1595], *Julius Caesar* [1599], *Hamlet* [1599–1601], *Troilus and Cressida* [1602], *Othello* [1602–04], *King Lear* [1604–05], *Macbeth* [1606], *Timon of Athens* [1607], *Antony and Cleopatra* [1606–07], and *Coriolanus* [1608]); romances (*Pericles, Prince of Tyre* [1606–08], *Cymbeline* [1609–10], *The Winter's Tale* [1610–11], and *The Tempest* [1611]). However, Shakespeare willfully defied the canons of classical drama by mingling comedy, tragedy, and history, so that in some cases classification is debatable or arbitrary.

Shakespeare's reputation, while subject to many fluctuations, was firmly established by the eighteenth century. Samuel Johnson remarked: "Perhaps it would not be easy to find any authour, except Homer, who invented so much as Shakespeare, who so much advanced the studies which he cultivated, who effused so much novelty upon his age or country. The form, the characters, the language, and the shows of the English drama are his." Early in the nineteenth century Samuel Taylor Coleridge declared: "The Englishman who without reverence, a proud and affectionate reverence, can utter the name of William Shakespeare, stands disqualified for the office of critic. . . . Great as was the genius of Shakespeare, his judgment was at least equal to it."

A curious controversy developed in the middle of the nineteenth century in regard to the authorship of Shakespeare's plays, some contending that Sir Francis Bacon was the actual author of the plays, others (including Mark Twain) advancing the claims of the earl of Oxford. None of these attempts has succeeded in persuading the majority of scholars that Shakespeare himself is not the author of the plays attributed to him.

In recent years many landmark editions of Shakespeare, with increasingly accurate texts and astute critical commentary, have emerged. These include the *Arden Shakespeare* (1951–), *The Oxford Shakespeare* (1982–), and *The New Cambridge Shakespeare* (1984–). Such critics as T. S. Eliot, G. Wilson Knight, Northrop Frye, W. H. Auden, and many others have continued to elucidate Shakespeare, his work, and his times, and he remains the most written-about author in the history of English literature. ❖

Thematic and Structural Analysis

Henry IV, Part One begins with Henry's description of himself as wearied by the act of ruling (**Act I, scene 1**). He states his intentions to mount a crusade to the Holy Land as penance for the murder of Richard II, a death for which Henry is responsible. His plans are disrupted by news of unrest on the borders of the kingdom, however, and he decides the crusade will have to wait. For the English are now battling both the Welsh, led by Glendower, and the Scottish, led by Douglas. Not only is Henry beset with political woes, but he is also worried about his son, Prince Henry (Harry), or Hal, who spends most of his time with a crowd of ne'er-do-wells led by Sir Jack Falstaff. The king is disgusted with Hal's behavior and compares his son to Lord Percy, also named Harry, but called Hotspur because of his impatience. Hotspur, who has been fighting the Scottish for Henry, is brave and chivalrous—more princely, in Henry's opinion. Henry wistfully thinks that perhaps Hal and Hotspur were switched at birth; he envies Northumberland, Hotspur's father. Thus at the play's opening, Henry has debts, political enemies, and a son he does not think he can trust, and he fears that the death of Richard II has brought all this down on his head, making him responsible for his own woes.

Hal does not live by the code of chivalry and bravery that Hotspur does, but he is not as dissolute as everyone believes him to be, as is revealed in the next scene (**I.2**). In this scene Hal (who will become Henry V) plots with Sir John Falstaff to rob highway travelers, a prank they seem to have played before. They talk in prose rather than in poetry, and their conversation is marked by teasing and bawdy jokes. When Falstaff exits, the crowd of ne'er-do-wells complicates the scheme, with Poins suggesting a double-plot: After Falstaff, Bardolph, Peto, and Gadshill rob the travelers, Hal and Poins will rob Falstaff, so that they can later hear his lying protestations about how he was beset by numerous bandits. Hal agrees to the plan, and Poins exits, leaving Hal to the speech that reveals his calculating character: He says he will imitate the sun, which, after a long time hiding behind "base contagious" clouds, is all the more "wondered at / By breaking through the foul and ugly mists." He will continue to behave as he has, waiting for the appropriate moment when his "reformation, glitt'ring o'er [his] fault, / Shall show more goodly and attract more eyes / Than that which hath no foil to set it off." His father, Hal thinks, will be all the more pleased and grateful when Hal suddenly reforms than if Hal had always behaved appropriately. This speech also reveals that Hal has every intention of one day ascending the throne and that he will redeem himself in the eyes of others when it is prudent to do so.

The next scene (**I.3**) concerns Hotspur, Hal's counterpoint and the representative of an archaic mode of chivalry. In an audience with Henry, Hotspur, who has just returned from battle and brought Scottish prisoners of war with him, refuses to give them up to the king unless Henry will ransom Mortimer (Hotspur's brother-in-law). Mortimer had led English troops against the Welsh leader, Glendower, had been captured, but had subsequently married Glendower's daughter. Henry refuses, calling Mortimer a traitor. The real reason for his refusal, however, is that Mortimer may have a more legitimate claim to the throne than does Henry himself, a claim that Hotspur and his father, Northumberland, think is valid. Henry demands Hotspur's prisoners, but Hotspur continues to refuse. Warning Northumberland and Hotspur of the consequences of continued refusal, the king exits.

After the king leaves, Hotspur, Northumberland, and Worcester (Northumberland's younger brother) discuss their problems with "this ingrate and cankered Bolingbroke" (a name for Henry IV in *Richard II,* before he was king). Hotspur challenges his uncle and father for being so subordinate to Henry, when it was with their help that he gained the throne in the first place:

> [S]hall it be that you set the crown
> Upon the head of this forgetful man,
> And for his sake wear the detested blot
> Of murderous subornation . . . ?

His challenge comes in typically hyperbolic language: Hotspur is neither patient nor diplomatic. He claims that it would be "an easy leap / To pluck bright honor from the pale-faced moon," in righting the wrong of enthroning Henry. Worcester and Northumberland manage to calm him down enough to sketch out the elements of a rebellion plot, in which Hotspur will convince his Scottish prisoners—and their leader, Douglas—to fight against Henry. Northumberland will meanwhile persuade the archbishop of York, Lord Scroop; Worcester will convince Owen Glendower, leader of the Welsh; and all three groups will then march against Henry. Thus Act I establishes three parallel plots, although they vary in gravity: unrest on the borders; Hal's scheme to rob the travelers and Falstaff; and Hotspur's plan to rebel against the king.

Act I also sets up the ongoing comparison between Hal and Hotspur: They are played off one another to illustrate the various princely qualities each possesses. Hotspur, however, is too impetuous ever to be a good king, as the play will make clear. Hal, on the other hand, has his father's political shrewdness, as evidenced in his earlier soliloquy. The rules of statecraft have changed: It is no longer possible for a Hotspur figure to prevail. His sword is no match for the cleverness of a Henry.

In **Act II, scene 1**, we see the workers and drinkers at the tavern Falstaff and Hal frequent; their bawdy jokes and insults echo the pattern of Falstaff's conversations with Hal. We cut to the next scene (**II.2**), in which Falstaff and his band rob the travelers and then are set upon by Hal and Poins, disguised in buckram (a stiff fabric). Falstaff, as expected, runs away, as do the others, leaving their booty behind. In a swift change of mood, we next go to Hotspur's estate at Warkworth Castle (**II.3**), where Hotspur's wife, Lady Percy, is trying to find out why he has been so distant and unaffectionate. "What is it," she asks, "that takes from thee / Thy stomach, pleasure, and thy golden sleep?" Hotspur is concentrating on the rebellion plot and refuses to tell her any details, for both her safety and his. The exchange between them is teasing and affectionate, however, with Lady Percy calling her husband a "mad-headed ape" and a little parrot. Their feelings for each other suggest that, despite Hotspur's intense focus on abstract concepts of honor, duty, and bravery, he is capable of deep emotion.

Back at the Boar's Head Tavern in Eastcheap (**II.4**), Hal and Poins have fun teasing the barkeep and then poke fun at Falstaff about the robbery. As they expected, he lies about his cowardice, saying first he was attacked by two men, then four, then seven, and finally eleven men. Hal tells Falstaff he knows that Falstaff is lying, calling him a "bed-presser," a "horse-backbreaker," and a "huge hill of flesh." But Falstaff counters— in turn calling the prince an "eelskin" and a "bull's pizzle"—by saying that of course he knew it was Hal who attacked him, but that he could not defend himself: "[W]as it for me to kill the heir apparent?" These scenes in Eastcheap are notable not only for their humor, but also for their presentation of English life: In portraying both the life at court and the life of the common people, the play gains in depth and scope of vision. When the king sends word that Hal must join him to defend against the rebels, Hal and Falstaff take turns rehearsing what Hal can say to his father. When Hal plays the king, he describes his son's companion, Falstaff, as "that father ruffian," to which Falstaff (acting the part of Hal) replies that the "king" should banish all Hal's drinking companions except "sweet Jack Falstaff, kind Jack Falstaff, true Jack Falstaff." For, he says, "banish plump Jack, and banish all the world." Revealingly, however, Hal replies, "I do, I will," which suggests that Hal, once on the throne, will not tolerate Falstaff's company. This reconfirms the intentions Hal expressed in his first soliloquy: that he will eventually take on the princely role expected of him.

Act III opens at Glendower's castle in Wales, where the rebels—Hotspur, Glendower, Mortimer, and Worcester—are discussing how they will divide the kingdom among themselves after they win the war. Glendower reveals himself to be superstitious and is mocked by Hotspur; the latter's impatience and barbed comments make Glendower angry, and Mortimer has to intercede for the conversation to continue. Hotspur protests that his share of the kingdom is smaller than the rest and declares that he will reroute the flow of a river in order to give himself more land, a statement that puts Glendower even more on edge. Glendower exits, saying he will join them on the battlefield in less than two weeks, and Mortimer and Worcester then chide Hotspur for his

[d]efect of manners, want of government,
Pride, haughtiness, opinion, and disdain,
The least of which haunting a nobleman
Loseth men's hearts and leaves behind a stain
Upon the beauty of all parts besides,
Beguiling them of commendation.

Lady Percy and Mortimer's wife (Glendower's daughter) enter, and Mortimer laments that he does not speak Welsh, which is the only language his wife speaks; he rests his head in her lap, and she sings him a song. Hotspur and his wife gently mock them, duplicating their pose, and again create an impression of a loving couple.

Act III, scene 2, brings Henry and Hal together in a confrontation. The king berates his son for being a wastrel and asks him if he can be trusted to take Henry's side in the upcoming fight. Henry warns Hal of losing his "princely privilege with vile participation," warning him that constant interaction with "rude society" will cause him to lose his royal authority, should he ever gain the throne. Henry reminds Hal of his own circumspect behavior, in language that resembles Hal's thoughts in his speech from Act I. Henry says he kept his person "fresh and new, ne'er seen but wondered at," and advises Hal to do the same. Weeping, Henry goes on to admire Hotspur, implicitly comparing him, as a "Mars in swathling clothes," with Hal, a comparison in which Hal falls far short. Hal pledges to become more princely in his behavior, which pleases the king tremendously. Hal's promise is slightly disingenuous, however, because, as we have seen from Act I, he always planned to assume a more princely demeanor when it seemed appropriate.

What we realize is that we are being given a portrayal of a prince poised between two fathers: Henry and Falstaff, each of whom can teach him something. On the one hand are Falstaff's sensuality and hedonism, shrewdness and wit, and on the other are Henry's political responsibility and acute sense of statecraft. Hal will ultimately choose between them, and although he chooses Henry's path, he will be a better king because of his knowledge of, and affection for, the people. Falstaff gives Hal that knowledge and experience, while Henry urges responsibility and political awareness. By combining the two, Hal will become a more effective ruler than his father. This choice suggests that an underlying question posed by the play is, What makes a good ruler? How can the disorder in the kingdom be brought to rights? As if to underscore that Hal is flanked by these two father figures, in **Act III, scene 3**, we move from Hal and his father to Falstaff and Bardolph at the Boar's Head. Hal enters to tell Falstaff that they are marching to battle and that Falstaff has been given command of an infantry division. "The land is burning," he says in his new, more princely, persona. "Percy stands on high, / And either we or they must lower lie."

Act IV, scene 1 brings us to the battlefield, and to Hotspur's camp. We learn that Northumberland is sick and cannot join the fighting, an announcement that should make Hotspur uneasy, because he needs his father's support. He turns his father's temporary absence to advantage, however: "If we without his help can make a head / To push against a kingdom, with his help / We shall o'erturn it topsy-turvy down." The news of Northumberland's illness is followed by the announcement that Glendower will not be able to draw together his troops for fourteen more days. Neither Douglas nor Hotspur seems to mind this news greatly, however. Hotspur is impatient to begin fighting; he is not even worried by the news that Prince Hal has joined his father's cause, being convinced that Hal is a wastrel, a "madcap" prince. We see his attitude toward the impending battle in the phrase "die all, die merrily," a marked contrast to Falstaff's blatant cowardice and Henry's measured consideration of the consequences of war.

Falstaff's harsher, more realistic perspective on war is the focus of the next scene (**IV.2**). He tells Hal that his men are just "food for powder, food for powder," meaning, of course, that they will march into battle and die. There is no glory in death, according to Falstaff. He presents a view of honor in opposition to Hotspur, for whom honor (the chivalric code, which at this point is becoming an anachronism) is the only thing worth fighting or dying for; in Falstaff's mind, nothing is worth dying for, and honor is an empty phrase. Falstaff lives for sensual pleasures—food, drink, sex—but in his sensuality is a kind of nihilism: Nothing has any meaning, ultimately, beyond his own pleasures.

We cut back to Hotspur's camp in **Act IV, scene 3** (this swift switching back and forth will continue for the rest of the play). Hotspur is eager to march on the king, as is Douglas, although the others advise waiting until morning, when their forces will be rested and more battle-ready. When Sir Walter Blunt enters with a message from Henry for a parley, Hotspur tells him the reason for the rebellion: Henry, in the eyes of Hotspur and his father, has "committed wrong on wrong," beginning with dethroning and then killing Richard II. Hotspur and Northumberland see Mortimer, earl of March, as rightful heir to Richard II, and Henry's refusal to ransom Mortimer from Glendower is another reason for their rebellion. Hotspur's speech is a litany of woes, but Blunt's response is a laconic "Shall I return this answer to the King?" Hotspur checks his temper and tells Blunt that his uncle will meet with the king in the morning.

The next scene (**IV.4**), in York, suggests that Hotspur might be wise to accept the king's offer of peace, but he is not present to hear the conversation. In this brief dialogue between the archbishop of York and Sir Michael (a member of his household), the archbishop gives voice to what others (including Glendower) might be thinking: "I fear the power of Percy is too weak / To wage an instant trial with the King." The absence of Northumberland, Mortimer, and Glendower, who are all supposed to fight with Hotspur and Douglas, seems too great an omission, in the archbishop's mind. **Act V** begins in the king's camp at Shrewsbury, with Henry, Hal, his brother (Lord John of Lancaster), Sir Walter Blunt, and Falstaff waiting for Hotspur's uncle, Worcester, to arrive. Henry welcomes Worcester, asking him to "unknit / This churlish knot of all-abhorred war, / And move in that obedient orb again, / where [he] did give a fair and natural light," implying that the rebellion has disrupted the natural order. Worcester reminds Henry that they were once friends but that Henry has broken faith in pursuit of his own ambitions. Hal steps in with praise for Hotspur and an admission that he himself has been "a truant to chivalry." To "save the blood on either side," Hal offers to fight Hotspur in single combat, a princely act but one the king forbids immediately. Henry tells Worcester that he will pardon everyone involved in the rebellion if they will disband, and Worcester exits. Hal is dubious that Hotspur will accept, because he knows that "Douglas and the Hotspur both together / Are confident against the world in arms." After the king and Hal exit, Falstaff remains onstage, meditating on the nature of honor. For Falstaff, honor is only a word, useless to those who die with it, and mere "air" to the living. Therefore, he says, "I'll none of it," and with that he exits.

The next scene (**V.2**) begins with Vernon and Worcester discussing the king's offer near the rebel camp. Vernon wants to tell Hotspur exactly what Henry said, but Worcester refuses because he does not believe the king will keep his word—or, if he keeps his word this time, he will simply wait and "find a time to punish this offense in other faults." Worcester thinks that although Hotspur himself might be forgiven, Henry will find a way to blame Worcester and Northumberland for Hotspur's rashness, which has "the excuse of youth and heat of blood." Vernon accedes, letting Worcester tell Hotspur that the king called them all traitors and summoned them to battle. Worcester does tell Hotspur of Hal's offer of single combat, which Hotspur at once suspects is an act of contempt. But Vernon quickly repeats Hal's praise of Hotspur, adding that if Hal were to mend his ways he would be "so sweet a hope" for England. The scene ends with messengers announcing that the battle is to begin, and Hotspur says,

> [I]f we live, we live to tread on kings;
> If die, brave death, when princes die with us!
> Now for our consciences, the arms are fair,
> When the intent of bearing them is just.

Hotspur does not realize that his mode of chivalry and honor at all costs is outmoded in this more political age, when honor matters less than politics—a lesson Hal has already mastered.

We cut to the battlefield (**V.3**), with Blunt and Douglas engaged in fighting. Blunt is dressed as Henry (as are many others, to act as decoys during the fighting), and Douglas kills him, believing he has killed the king. Hotspur enters, praising Douglas's bravery, but recognizes the face as Blunt's. Douglas resolves to kill all the kings he sees on the battlefield, and they exit. Falstaff enters, alone, lamenting that almost all his 150 men are dead. Hal enters and sees Blunt's body; Falstaff, lying, tells him that he has already avenged Blunt's death. Hal reaches for Falstaff's pistol and pulls out a bottle of sack from the holster; disgusted, he marches off. Falstaff closes this scene also, again presenting his own interpretation of honorable behavior on the battlefield: He would rather be alive than have such "grinning honor as Sir Walter [Blunt] hath."

Act V, scene 4 continues the battle, now with Douglas and Henry fighting, although Douglas is not sure if Henry is, in fact, really the king. Douglas gains the upper hand, but Hal enters and attacks Douglas so fiercely that he flees. Hal's rescue of Henry shows his acceptance of his princely role; he is behaving honorably, but without Hotspur's overzealousness. Henry forgives Hal his past behavior—"Thou hast redeemed thy lost opinion"—and sees that Hal is indeed his rightful son. The king exits and Hotspur enters: The two Harrys are finally face-to-face, and Hal says,

> [T]hink not, Percy,
> To share with me in glory any more.
> Two stars keep not their motion in one sphere,
> Nor can one England brook a double reign
> Of Harry Percy and the Prince of Wales.

As they begin to fight, Falstaff and Douglas enter and also engage in battle. Falstaff falls down as if dead, Douglas exits, and Hal kills Hotspur.

Hal is left standing onstage, flanked by the bodies of Falstaff and Hotspur, physical representation of the choice Hal has had to make between Falstaff's sensual life and Hotspur's chivalry. His choice is clear when he eulogizes Hotspur's courage and "great heart" but only passingly comments on Falstaff, saying that he would miss Falstaff more if he were still "much in love with vanity." He departs the stage, and Falstaff stands up, rationalizing his feigned death by saying that "the better part of valor is discretion, in which the better part I have saved my own life." He then plunges his dagger into Hotspur's thigh and lifts the dead body onto his shoulders to carry him away. Hal and John of Lancaster return to the stage; Hal is astounded to see Falstaff alive, and even more so to hear Falstaff's elaborate story of how he himself killed Percy, a lie the prince allows. The three of them hear a trumpet play a retreat, signalling that Henry's forces have won.

The final scene (**V.5**) gathers Henry, Hal, Lord John, and Westmoreland together, with Vernon and Worcester as their prisoners. Henry chastises Worcester for not truthfully relaying his message to Douglas and Hotspur, but Worcester is unrepentant. Henry commands that Worcester and Vernon be killed, and they are led away. Douglas is a prisoner in Hal's tent, and Hal sends his brother to set Douglas free as a tribute to his valor—another princely act. The play ends with Henry laying plans for the next battle: Lord John and Westmoreland will lead half the army to meet Northumberland, while the king and Hal will march toward Wales to fight Glendower.

Henry IV, Part One thus presents a kingdom in turmoil, a kingdom in search of a ruler. The death of Richard II is an act for which Henry is responsible; Henry's ascent to the throne becomes a usurpation, an evil act that brings about the disruption in the kingdom. This disruption is made manifest not only in Hotspur's rebellion, but also in the disorder and dissolution of Eastcheap. Both contribute to the delinquency of the kingdom, in Henry's eyes. He thinks of Hotspur's plot and Hal's wild behavior as his punishments for Richard's death. Thus Hal's acceptance of his true princely role suggests that eventually order in the kingdom will be restored. However, part one ends with only half the problem solved: The rebels have been more or less defeated, but Falstaff is still very much alive. Hal's full character, the lessons he has learned from both his "fathers," Falstaff and Henry, will become fully evident in *Henry V*.

Further, in the comparisons between Hotspur and Hal, Shakespeare presents the struggle between the old chivalric order and the new order marked by political strategies and intrigue. Hotspur is not an unsympathetic character; in fact he is rather appealing. He is, however, old-fashioned. Hal's ability to take on the language and demeanor of his surroundings marks him as a survivor and as a man who will eventually rule with both might and brains. ❖

—*Deborah Williams*
Iona College

List of Characters

Henry IV came to power in the play *Richard II* through a combination of political intrigue and rebellion; after he ascended the throne, he had Richard killed, an act that, in *Henry IV, Part One,* throws into question his right to the crown. Henry is troubled by the behavior of his son Hal and by political unrest in the kingdom. He is not a particularly warm character, but his political shrewdness is a lesson Hal must learn.

Henry ("Hal") is Henry IV's oldest son, the Prince of Wales. Although he will one day rule England, he spends his time with Sir John Falstaff, drinking and carousing, which causes everyone in the play to underestimate his abilities. Hal himself knows this is what people think, as demonstrated in his soliloquy in Act I, in which he says that at the right time he will change his behavior and surprise everyone. Hal must choose between the model offered by Falstaff and the model offered by his father; his choice implicitly poses the question of what makes a good ruler. Hal represents the new order; he combines political awareness with the common touch. He also must choose between the different visions of life offered by Falstaff and by Hotspur.

Sir John Falstaff is Hal's constant companion. Falstaff and his friends, all regulars at the Boar's Head Tavern in Eastcheap, are the companions that worry King Henry. Falstaff lives for pleasure, particularly food and drink. His disdain for honor and bravery put him in marked contrast to Hotspur, with whom Hal is constantly compared. Falstaff's instinct for self-preservation at all costs is demonstrated in humorous situations, as when Hal robs him, but also on the battlefield, where he plays dead to save his life. His pleasure-seeking attitude is solipsistic in the extreme: Nothing means anything to Falstaff unless it directly affects him.

Henry Percy ("Hotspur"), a member of the Percy family, who helped put Henry on the throne but are now disgruntled with Henry's behavior, is Hal's counterpoint. Where Hal appears dissolute and uninterested in the condition of the state, Hotspur is vitally interested. But Hotspur is concerned only with honor and questions of chivalry; he gets what he wants by fighting rather than by thinking. The fight between Hal and Hotspur is the fight between the new order and the old; both men have princely qualities, but Hal is able to unify bravery with strategy and cunning, which Hotspur, as his name suggests, is too impatient to do. Hotspur is not an unsympathetic character; he is simply a character whose admirable qualities are outdated.

Henry Percy, earl of Northumberland, is Hotspur's father and one of the rebellion leaders. Henry IV admits to being jealous of Northumberland because Hotspur is, at least in the first three acts of the play, a more princely character than Hal.

Archibald, earl of Douglas, another rebel leader, is as impatient for battle as Hotspur. Douglas fights so valiantly during the battle that although he is captured, Hal has him set free as a tribute to his valor.

Edmund Mortimer, earl of March, is fighting the Welsh when he is captured by Glendower. He marries Glendower's daughter and joins the rebel forces; it is Henry's refusal to ransom Mortimer that initially triggers Hotspur's anger.

Owen Glendower is the leader of the Welsh tribes and a co-conspirator; he and Northumberland work together to try to curb Hotspur's impatience.

Poins, Gadshill, Peto, Bardolph are all friends of Hal's who frequent the Boar's Head Tavern with Falstaff. ✤

Critical Views

[John Dryden (1631–1700), aside from being the greatest English poet of the later seventeenth century, was a
pioneer in literary criticism. Among his important critical works are *Of Heroick Plays* (1672) and *Of Dramatick
Poesie* (1668), from which the following extract is
taken. Here, Dryden argues that Shakespeare drew the
portrait of Falstaff by mingling several different
"humours" or personality traits.]

I am assur'd from diverse persons, that *Ben. Johnson* was actually acquainted with such a man, one altogether as ridiculous
as he (Morose in *The Silent Woman*) is here represented.
Others say it is not enough to find one man of such an humour;
it must be common to more, and the more common the more
natural. To prove this they instance in the best of Comical
Characters, *Falstaff:* There are many men resembling him; Old,
Fat, Merry, Cowardly, Drunken, Amorous, Vain and Lying: But
to convince these people I need but tell them, that humour is
the ridiculous extravagance of conversation, wherein one man
differs from all others. If then it be common or communicated
to many, how differs it from other mens? or what indeed causes it to be ridiculous so much as the singularity of it? As for
Falstaff, he is not properly one humour, but a Miscellany of
Humours or Images, drawn from so many several men; that
wherein he is singular in his wit, or those things he sayes,
praeter expectatum, unexpected by the Audience; his quick
evasions when you imagine him supriz'd, which as they are
extreamly diverting of themselves, so receive a great addition
from his person; for the very sight of such an unwieldy old
debauch'd fellow is a Comedy alone.
> —John Dryden, *Of Dramatick Poesie: An Essay* (London: Henry
> Herringman, 1668), pp. 51–52

[Samuel Johnson (1709–1784), perhaps the greatest British literary figure of the eighteenth century, was a poet, novelist, critic, and biographer of distinction. In 1765 he wrote a monograph, *Preface to His Edition of Shakespeare,* and in that same year he edited a landmark annotated edition of Shakespeare's works, still highly regarded for the astuteness of its commentary. In this extract, taken from the notes to his edition, Johnson confesses to finding the character of Falstaff engaging in spite of his rascally nature.]

But Falstaff unimitated, unimitable Falstaff, how shall I describe thee? Thou compound of sense and vice; of sense which may be admired but not esteemed, of vice which may be despised, but hardly detested. Falstaff is a character loaded with faults, and with those faults which naturally produce contempt. He is a thief, and a glutton, a coward, and a boaster, always ready to cheat the weak, and prey upon the poor; to terrify the timorous and insult the defenceless. At once obsequious and malignant, he satirises in their absence those whom he lives by flattering. He is familiar with the Prince only as an agent of vice, but of this familiarity he is so proud as not only to be supercilious and haughty with common men, but to think his interest of importance to the Duke of Lancaster. Yet the man thus corrupt, thus despicable, makes himself necessary to the prince that despises him, by the most pleasing of all qualities, perpetual gaiety, by an unfailing power of exciting laughter, which is the more freely indulged, as his wit is not of the splendid or ambitious kind, but consists in easy escapes and sallies of levity, which make sport but raise no envy. It must be observed that he is stained with no enormous or sanguinary crimes, so that his licentiousness is not so offensive but that it may be borne for his mirth.

The moral to be drawn from this representation is, that no man is more dangerous than he that with a will to corrupt, hath the power to please; and that neither wit nor honesty ought to think themselves safe with such a companion when they see Henry seduced by Falstaff.

—Samuel Johnson, *The Plays of William Shakespeare* (London: J. & R. Tonson, 1768), Vol. 4, p. 355

MAURICE MORGANN ON THE FLAWS AND VIRTUES OF FALSTAFF

[Maurice Morgann (1726–1802) was a pioneering Shakespeare critic who, aside from various political and literary tracts, wrote the important monograph, *An Essay on the Dramatic Character of Sir John Falstaff* (1777), from which the following extract is taken. Here, Morgann, adopting the critical stance that Falstaff was a real person, ruminates over both his flaws and virtues.]

To me then it appears that the leading quality in *Falstaff*'s character, and that from which all the rest take their colour, is a high degree of wit and humour, accompanied with great natural vigour and alacrity of mind. This quality so accompanied, led him probably very early into life, and made him highly acceptable to society; so acceptable, as to make it seem unnecessary for him to acquire any other virtue. Hence, perhaps, his continued debaucheries and dissipations of every kind.—He seems, by nature, to have had a mind free of malice or any evil principle; but he never took the trouble of acquiring any good one. He found himself esteemed and beloved with all his faults; nay *for* his faults, which were all connected with humour, and for the most part, grew out of it. As he had, possibly, no vices but such as he thought might be openly professed, so he appeared more dissolute thro' ostentation. To the character of wit and humour, to which all his other qualities seem to have conformed themselves, he appears to have added a very necessary support, *that* of the profession of a *Soldier*. He had from nature, as I presume to say, a spirit of boldness and enterprise; which in a Military age, tho' employment was only occasional, kept him always above contempt, secured him an honourable reception among the Great, and suited best both with his particular mode of humour and of vice. Thus living continually in society, nay even in Taverns, and indulging himself, and being indulged by others, in every debauchery; drinking, whoring, gluttony, and ease; assuming a liberty of fiction, necessary perhaps to his wit, and often falling into falsity and lies, he seems to have set, by degrees, all sober reputation at defiance; and finding eternal resources in his wit, he borrows, shifts, defrauds, and even robs, without dishonour.—Laughter and approbation attend his greatest excesses; and being governed visibly by no settled bad principle or ill design, fun and humour account for and cover all. By degrees, however, and thro' indulgence, he acquires bad habits, becomes an humourist, grows enormously corpulent, and falls into the infirmities of age; yet never quits, all the time, one single levity or vice of youth, or loses any of that cheerfulness of mind, which had enabled him to pass thro' this course with ease to himself and delight to others; and thus, at last, mixing youth and age, enterprize and corpulency, wit and folly, poverty and expence, title and buffoonery, innocence as to purpose, and wickedness as to practice; neither incurring hatred by bad principle, or contempt by Cowardice, yet involved in circumstances productive of imputation in both; a butt and a wit, a humourist and a man of humour, a touchstone and a laughing stock, a jester and a jest, has Sir *John Falstaff,* taken at that period in his life in which we see him, become the most perfect Comic character that perhaps ever was exhibited.

—Maurice Morgann, An Essay on the Dramatic Character of Sir John Falstaff (London: T. Davies, 1777), pp. 17–20

A. C. BRADLEY ON UNDERSTANDING FALSTAFF

[A. C. Bradley (1851–1935) was the leading British Shakespeare scholar of his time. He taught at the

University of Liverpool, the University of Glasgow, and at Oxford University, and wrote a celebrated book, *Shakespearean Tragedy* (1904), as well as *Oxford Lectures on Poetry* (1909), and *A Miscellany* (1929). In this extract, Bradley comments on the complexities of Falstaff's character.]

The bliss of freedom gained in humour is the essence of Falstaff. His humour is not directed only or chiefly against obvious absurdities; he is the enemy of everything that would interfere with his ease, and therefore of anything serious, and especially of everything respectable and moral. For these things impose limits and obligations, and make us the subjects of old father antic the law, and the catagorical imperative, and our station and its duties, and conscience, and reputation, and other people's opinions, and all sorts of nuisances. I say he is therefore their enemy; but I do him wrong; to say that he is their enemy implies that he regards them as serious and recognises their power, when in truth he refuses to recognise them at all. They are to him absurd; and to reduce a thing *ad absurdum* is to reduce it to nothing and to walk about free and rejoicing. This is what Falstaff does with all the would-be serious things of life, sometimes only by his words, sometimes by his actions too. He will make truth appear absurd by solemn statements, which he utters with perfect gravity and which he expects nobody to believe; and honour, by demonstrating that it cannot set a leg, and that neither the living nor the dead can possess it; and law, by evading all the attacks of its highest representative and almost forcing him to laugh at his own defeat; and patriotism, by filling his pockets with the bribes offered by competent soldiers who want to escape service, while he takes in their stead the halt and maimed and the gaol-birds; and duty, by showing how he labours in his vocation—of theiving; and courage, alike by mocking at his own capture of Colvile and gravely claiming to have killed Hotspur; and war, by offering the Prince his bottle of sack when he is asked for a sword; and religion, by amusing himself with remorse at odd times when he has nothing else to do; and the fear of death, by maintaining perfectly untouched, in the face of peril and even while he *feels* the fear of death, the very same power of dissolving it in persiflage that he shows when he sits at ease in his inn. These are the wonderful achievements which he performs, not with the sourness of a cynic, but with the gaiety of a boy. And, therefore, we praise him, we laud him, for he offends none but the virtuous, and denies that life is real or life is earnest, and delivers us from the oppression of such nightmares, and lifts us into the atmosphere of perfect freedom.

No one in the play understands Falstaff fully, any more than Hamlet was understood by the persons round him. They are both men of genius. Mrs. Quickly and Bardolph are his slaves, but they know not why. 'Well, fare thee well,' says the hostess whom he has pillaged and forgiven; 'I have known thee these twenty-nine years, come peas-cod time, but an honester and truer-hearted man—well, fare thee well.' Poins and the Prince delight in him; they get him into corners for the pleasure of seeing him escape in ways they cannot imagine; but they often take him much too seriously. Poins, for instance, rarely sees, the Prince does not always see, and moralising critics never see, that when Falstaff speaks ill of a companion behind his back, or writes to the Prince that Poins spreads it abroad that the Prince is to marry his sister, he knows quite well that what he says will be repeated, or rather, perhaps, is absolutely indifferent whether it be repeated or not, being certain that it can only give him an opportunity for humour. It is the same with his lying, and almost the same with his cowardice, the two main vices laid to his charge even by sympathisers. Falstaff is neither a liar nor a coward in the usual sense, like the typical cowardly boaster of comedy. He tells his lies either for their own humour, or on purpose to get himself into a difficulty. He rarely expects to be believed, perhaps never. He abandons a statement or contradicts it the moment it is made. There is scarcely more intent in his lying than in the humorous exaggerations which he pours out in soliloquy just as much as when others are by. Poins and the Prince understand this in part. You see them waiting eagerly to convict him, not that they may really put him to shame, but in order to enjoy the greater lie that will swallow up the less. But their sense of humour lags behind his. Even the Prince seems to accept as half-serious that remorse of his which passes so suddenly into glee at the idea of taking a purse, and his request to his friend to bestride him if he should see him down in the battle. Bestride Falstaff! 'Hence! Wilt thou lift up Olympus?'

—A. C. Bradley, "The Rejection of Falstaff" (1902), *Oxford Lectures on Poetry* (London: Macmillan, 1909), pp. 262–64

WYNDHAM LEWIS ON THE CHARACTERISTICS OF FALSTAFF

[Wyndham Lewis (1882–1957), whose career was advanced partly by his friend Ezra Pound, was the author of modernist novels (including *The Apes of God,* 1930) and a leading figure in the vorticist movement, which attacked the sentimentality of nineteenth-century art. Among his critical works are *Time and Western Man* (1927) and *The Lion and the Fox* (1927). In this extract of the latter work, Lewis ponders the characteristics of Falstaff.]

In Falstaff, Shakespeare has given us a very interesting specimen indeed of consummate worldliness, with a very powerfully developed humorous proclivity, which served him better than any suit of armour could in the various vicissitudes of his life. An excellent substitute even for a *shamanizing* faculty, and enabling its possessor to escape the inconveniences and conventional disgrace of being feminine—at the same it provides him with most of the social advantages of the woman. The sense of humour is from that point of view the masterpiece of worldly duplicity and strategy. On the field of battle at Tewkesbury, Falstaff avails himself of it in a famous scene, and gives us a classical exhibition of its many advantages, and the graceful operation of its deceit. It does not cut off its practitioner from "men" or the rough "hero type," but on the contrary endears him to them. So it becomes even a substitute for courage. There is no lack that it does not cover. With it Falstaff is as safe on the battlefield as the shamanized noble noticed by Percy Hotspur.

So if Falstaff is the embodiment of a mass of worldly expedient, this is of course all directed to defeating the reality as much as Don Quixote's. He is a walking disease, but his disease is used to evade the results of that absence of a sense of humour which is so conspicuous a characteristic of nature and natural phenomena. The sense of humour is woven into a magic carpet; with it he progresses through his turbulent career, bearing a charmed life. This "sense" performs for Falstaff the office of a psychological liberator; it is of magic potency, turning the field of Tewkesbury into a field of play, and cheating death wherever they meet. ⟨. . .⟩

Falstaff is a "man of wit and pleasure," and could generally be described as a very good specimen of a "man of the world." But the same thing applies to him as to Iago: the "man of the world" is never so dramatically and openly cynical as Falstaff, any more than he is so candid as Machiavelli. He is not dramatic at all. To come to one of the necessary conclusions in this connexion, if the *Machiavel* were an Englishman he would be like Falstaff. This laziness, rascality and "good fellow" quality, crafty in the brainless animal way, is the English way of being a "deep-brained Machiavel."

But Falstaff is a "child," too, a "*naif,*" as Ulrici says. A worldly mixture of any strength is never without that ingredient. The vast compendium of worldly bluff that is Falstaff would have to contain that. It was like "any christom child" that he "went away," Mistress Quickly says.

He is armed from head to foot with sly feminine inferiorities, lovable weaknesses and instinctively cultivated charm. He is a big helpless bag of guts exposing himself boldly to every risk on the child's, or the woman's, terms. When he runs away or lies down he is more adorable than any hero "facing fearful odds."

His immense girth and stature lends the greatest point, even, to his character. He is a hero run hugely to seed: he is actually heavier and bigger than the heaviest and biggest true colossus or hero. He is in that respect, physically, a mock-hero. Then this childishness is enhanced by his great physical scale, so much the opposite of the child's perquisite of smallness.

And because of this meaningless, unmasculine immensity he always occupies the centre of the stage, he is the great landmark in any scene where he is. It all means nothing, and is a physical sham and trick put on the eye. And so he becomes the embodiment of bluff and worldly practice, the colossus of the little.

> —Wyndham Lewis, "Falstaff," *The Lion and the Fox: The Role of the Hero in the Plays of Shakespeare* (London: Grant Richards, 1927), pp. 224, 226–27

HAROLD C. GODDARD ON HISTORICAL INTRIGUES IN *HENRY IV, PART ONE*

[Harold C. Goddard (1878–1950) was for many years head of the English department at Swarthmore University. He was the author of *Studies in New England Transcendentalism* (1906) and the editor of an edition of Ralph Waldo Emerson's essays (1926). In this extract, taken from his important book, *The Meaning of Shakespeare* (1951), Goddard examines the opening of *Henry IV, Part One* and the political intrigues that are the backbone of the play's historical drama.]

I Henry IV opens with a proclamation of peace and a definite proposal of the promised crusade to the sepulcher of Christ:

> To chase these pagans in those holy fields
> Over whose acres walk'd those blessed feet
> Which fourteen hundred years ago were nail'd
> For our advantage on the bitter cross.

It must have seemed to the pagans an odd way of instituting peace. But pagans of course did not count as human beings to Henry. There sounds, however, a note of something like genuine contrition in the reference to Christ. Yet, on his deathbed, Henry was to confess explicitly that this crusade was a purely political move to distract attention from civil unrest!

For the usual thing had happened. The men who helped Henry to the throne (the Percys) grew envious of the power they did not share and of his friendship:

> The king will always think him in our debt,
> And think we think ourselves unsatisfied,
> Till he hath found a time to pay us home.

This suspicion, reciprocated, led to acts on both sides that put foundations under it with the result that Henry's reign, where it was not open war, was incessant dissension.

Henry has no sooner declared the end of "civil butchery" in the opening speech of the play than a messenger from Wales enters announcing a thousand men "butcher'd" by the wild and irregular Glendower. And on the heels of this, news from Scotland: Hotspur has met and defeated the Scots. Ten thousand of them slain, and prisoners taken. But their captor refuses to hand them over to the King! This must be looked into. The pilgrimage to Jerusalem must be postponed.

A bit later the King confronts the Percys: father, son, and uncle. He declares that he has been too forbearing in the past, "smooth as oil, soft as young down," and implies that from now on he will demand the respect due him. Worcester bids him remember who helped him to his throne. To which the King retorts:

> Worcester, get thee gone; for I do see
> Danger and disobedience in thine eye.

The ghost of Richard again! Henry solving a problem by pushing it out of sight, doing to his enemy exactly what Richard did to him! The "buried fear" is stirring in its grave.

And the King's self-control is in for an even more severe jolt. Hotspur refuses to give up his prisoners unless his brother-in-law, Mortimer, who has been captured by the Welshman Glendower, shall be ransomed. At the mention of Mortimer something seems to explode inside the King:

> Let me not hear you speak of Mortimer;
> Send me your prisoners with the speediest means
> Or you shall hear in such a kind from me
> As will displease you.

Can this be Henry? The tone, so unlike him, shows that the name of Mortimer has touched something at the very foundation of his nature. When the King, in high dudgeon, has gone out, Worcester explains. Mortimer is legal heir to the throne: so by right, and so proclaimed by Richard. Of what avail to have had Richard murdered if his title transmigrated into a living man?

This is news to Hotspur. Mortimer! With the diabolic insight of a small boy who has hit on a scheme for teasing his sister, he dances about in an ecstasy and cries:

> I will find him when he lies asleep,
> And in his ear I'll holla "Mortimer!"
> Nay,
> I'll have a starling shall be taught to speak
> Nothing but "Mortimer," and give it him,
> To keep his anger still in motion.

Henry stands revealed to him for the hypocrite he is: a "vile politician," a "fawning greyhound," a "king of smiles."

Forthwith the three Percys hatch a plot to unite under themselves the Scots, the Welsh, and the Archbishop of York and, with Mortimer as the cutting edge, to defy the King. I said that three men, or even four, contend for the primacy in this play. And now we have a fifth. Mortimer is on the stage in only one scene. But he is the play's mainspring as certainly as is the Ghost in *Hamlet*. Shakespeare grew more and more fond of quietly suggesting the immense dramatic importance of figures partly or wholly behind the action, of making the absent present.

—Harold C. Goddard, *The Meaning of Shakespeare* (Chicago: University of Chicago Press, 1951), pp. 163–65

W. H. AUDEN ON FALSTAFF AND CHRISTIANITY

[W. H. Auden (1907–1973) was one of the leading British poets of the twentieth century as well as an important critic. His best critical work is contained in *The Dyer's Hand and Other Essays* (1962), which contains several essays on Shakespeare. In this extract, Auden explores Christian themes connected with Falstaff.]

Falstaff never really does anything, but he never stops talking, so that the impression he makes on the audience is not of idleness but of infinite energy. He is never tired, never bored, and until he is rejected he radiates happiness as Hal radiates power, and this happiness without apparent cause, this untiring devotion to making others laugh becomes a comic image for a love which is absolutely self-giving.

Laughing and loving have certain properties in common. Laughter is contagious but not, like physical force, irresistible. A man in a passion of any kind cannot be made to laugh; if he laughs, it is a proof that he has already mastered his passion. Laughter is an action only in a special sense. Many kinds of action can cause laughter, but the only kind of action that laughter causes is more laughter; while we laugh, time stops and no other kind of action can be contemplated. In rage or hysteria people are sometimes said to "laugh" but no one can confuse the noises they make with the sound of real laughter. Real laughter is absolutely unaggressive; we cannot wish people or things we find amusing to be other than they are; we do not desire them to change them, far less hurt or destroy them. An angry and dangerous mob is rendered harmless by the orator who can succeed in making it laugh. Real laughter is always, as we say, "disarming."

Falstaff makes the same impression on us that the Sinner of Lublin made upon his rabbi.

> In Lublin lived a great sinner. Whenever he went to talk to the rabbi, the rabbi readily consented and conversed with him as if he were a man of integrity and one who was a close friend. Many of the hassidim were annoyed at this and one said to the other: "Is it possible that our rabbi who has only to look once

into a man's face to know his life from first to last, to know the very origin of his soul, does not see that this fellow is a sinner? And if he does see it, that he considers him worthy to speak to and associate with." Finally they summoned up courage to go to the rabbi himself with their question. He answered them: "I know all about him as well as you. But you know how I love gaiety and hate dejection. And this man is so great a sinner. Others repent the moment they have sinned, are sorry for a moment, and then return to their folly. But he knows no regrets and no doldrums, and lives in his happiness as in a tower. And it is the radiance of his happiness that overwhelms my heart."

Falstaff's happiness is almost an impregnable tower, but not quite. "I am that I am" is not a complete self-description; he must also add—"The young prince hath misled me. I am the fellow with the great belly, and he is my dog."

The Christian God is not a self-sufficient being like Aristotle's First Cause, but a God who creates a world which he continues to love although it refuses to love him in return. He appears in this world, not as Apollo or Aphrodite might appear, disguised as man so that no mortal should recognize his divinity, but as a real man who openly claims to be God. And the consequence is inevitable. The highest religious and temporal authorities condemn Him as a blasphemer and a Lord of Misrule, as a Bad Companion for mankind. Inevitable because, as Richelieu said, "The salvation of State is in this world," and history has not as yet provided us with any evidence that the Prince of this world has changed his character.

—W. H. Auden, "The Prince's Dog" (1959), *The Dyer's Hand and Other Essays* (New York: Random House, 1962), pp. 206–8

M. M. Reese on Henry IV's Turbulent Reign

[M. M. Reese (1910–1987) was a lecturer, professor of English, and an editor of the literary journal *Encounter*. Among his publications are *Shakespeare: His World and His Work* (1953) and *William Shakespeare* (1963).

In this extract, Reese examines Henry IV's dashed hopes for peace.]

Henry is prematurely old, and he knows, none better, the reason why. His 'holy purpose to Jerusalem' acknowledges a weight of sin which this hallowed expedition possibly may lift. The aspiration was not hypocritical and not absurd. In mediaeval England, to dedicate oneself to the crusading ideal was believed to expiate all other crimes (even, so the chroniclers thought, the abnormal lusts of Richard I), and Henry hoped that at 'the sepulchre of Christ' he would find forgiveness for the sin of usurpation which had brought to nothing all his good intentions. In fact he was destined never to leave these shores; and his eventual death in the palace chamber called Jerusalem sharpens the irony and hopelessness of his predicament. Immediately, in the very first scene, his expectation of peace is dashed by the 'post from Wales loaden with heavy news' that Mortimer has fallen to Glendower; and his satisfaction in the victory over the Scots at Holmedon is turned to anger at the report of Hotspur's dangerous insolence in refusing to surrender his prisoners. Then private grief intrudes upon his official anxieties when he wishes for a son who would be 'the theme of honour's tongue' and not a tavern-hunting wastrel. The next scene reveals the Prince's low companions as themselves a symptom of the land's disorder—the image of the sun is asked to promise that, when he is king, the law shall wink at those who conduct their business by the light of the moon (I ii 26–33). It suggests, too, that Hal likes to associate with these dissolute men because there is something in the atmosphere of the court, with its thin-blooded care for the official proprieties, that stifles humanity. All the responsibility for the country's sickness fastens itself on Henry, who is trapped in the prison of his own misdeeds.

The third scene shows that he does not occupy it alone. Here he is in angry conflict with the Percies, his allies in the events that brought him to the throne. As Richard predicted, their common complicity in these events has now locked them in a struggle that will be fatal to the country and fatal to themselves. The Percies cannot forgive Henry for taking the richest prize: if he were to give them half the kingdom, Richard had said, they would think it too little, having helped him to win it all. The present relationship between them is therefore grounded in mutual fear: the Percies' fear that Henry, knowing them for what they are, will not rest until he has robbed them of their power to strike in the same way again; and Henry's corresponding fear that men who have been rebels once are likely to be rebels for evermore. It is a contest in which there can be no winners. Both sides are the helpless victims of their own past.

This sense of being borne along by necessity deepens as the play develops. In his first interview with his erring son (III ii) Henry tries to rouse him to his princely responsibilities, but the sum of his advice is merely to show how irrevocably the dangerous present is linked with what has happened in the past. Henry is sincerely anxious to see the country ruled in justice, peace and order, but the inescapable past always rises to prevent it. It is thrown in his teeth again when his offer of amnesty is refused before the battle at Shrewsbury. Worcester and Hotspur both recite their version of the events of 1399, and Worcester finally refuses to take Henry's offer to the rebel camp. He simply does not believe that the King would be able to fulfill its conditions:

> It is not possible, it cannot be,
> The King should keep his word in loving us;
> He will suspect us still, and find a time
> To punish this offence in other faults:
> Suspicion all our lives shall be stuck full of eyes;
> For treason is but trusted like the fox. . . .
> Look how we can, or sad or merrily,
> Interpretation will misquote our looks.   (V ii 4.)

—M. M. Reese, *The Cease of Majesty: A Study of Shakespeare's History Plays* (London: Edward Arnold, 1961), pp. 286–88

HUGH DICKINSON ON PRINCE HAL AND SHAKESPEARE'S USE OF TIME

[Hugh Dickinson is the author of *Myth on the Modern Stage* (1969). In this extract, Dickinson argues that Prince Hal's development is the central theme of *Henry IV, Part One*.]

If one sets out to stage the first part of Shakespeare's *Henry IV*, he finds it necessary to divorce the text from its related historical plays and regard it in strict isolation as "the book of the play", the basis for a dramatic, rather than a literary, experience. Such an approach must assume at the outset that the play is unified and complete in itself; that it will yield a coherent action, a core about which the playwright has organized its varied events. It must assume also that, despite the enormously diverse views of the play, its characters, structure, focus and theme, the text will provide answers that will hold in the theatre, or hold not at all. This is a reading of the play derived from the text in rehearsal and performance. It proposes the theatrical approach as a critical discipline having a valid claim to consideration, and presents a judgment of the play arrived at through the medium of the stage—for which, after all, it was expressly created.

In this reading, most of the answers will be found to lie in the actions of the character against whom critics have levelled some of their worst charges: namely, Henry, Prince of Wales. In performance, it is Hal who provides the clue to the total action, which is: to "redeem the time"; it is Hal whose reformation forms the core of the action, and who unifies and completes the play; it is Hal who is its protagonist and its unassuming hero, as well; it is Hal whose deeds most explicitly dramatize the theme of the play, which is: the education of a prince; and, finally, it is Hal who demonstrates the supreme attribute of kingship to be, not honor, but self-sacrifice.

Stanislawski's term for the total action of a play, "the super-objective", assumes that a good play is so organized that all its events are directed toward achieving a single, overriding objective; that everything in the play, in fact, combines to accomplish this desired end—including those forces that oppose it, but that actually help to bring it about in the long run.

The super-objective is: to redeem the time. The recurrence of the phrase itself, or its equivalent in action, is scarcely accidental in the various strands of the plot at the beginning of the play. It reminds one of the Epistle to the Ephesians, as if Shakespeare had had it in mind as his text: "See how you walk circumspectly, not as unwise, but as wise: redeeming the time, because the days are evil (v. 15–16)." A modern translation puts it more colloquially: "See to it that you walk with care: not as unwise but as wise, making the most of your time, because the days are evil." (Each of the three forces in the play that converge upon Prince Hal, and in regard to which he must define his position, illustrates this. The forces are the crown, the tavern, and the field, represented respectively by King Henry, Falstaff, and Hotspur.

The king seeks to redeem the time by uniting England in a crusade to the Holy Land, and thus to secure the throne against the threat of civil war (I.i). Events quickly thwart his aim, rob him of the initiative, and require him to deal instead with military and political conditions that jeopardize the crown.

The real premise of the play, therefore—that aim or decision which is to be tested and proved by all subsequent events— rests with Prince Hal. But Falstaff states it first, in comic terms, when he announces his intention, repeated throughout the play, of reforming altogether: "I must give over this life, and I will give it over. By the Lord, and I do not, I am a villain (I.ii. 83–84)." This use of ironic counterpoint anticipates Hal's serious resolve to reform, which provides the premise of the play, and which is expressed in his much-debated soliloquy:

> I know you all, and will awhile uphold
> The unyoked humour of your idleness.
> Yet herein will I imitate the sun . . . .
> So, when this loose behaviour I throw off
> And pay the debt I never promiséd,
> By how much better than my word I am,
> By so much shall I falsify men's hopes . . . .
> I'll so offend, to make offence a skill,
> Redeeming time when men think least I will. (I.ii. 171–193)

The super-objective is voiced again, this time by Hotspur, in the following scene. Stung by the king's refusal to ransom Mortimer, he threatens to join the latter and make war upon the king. Characteristically, he adjures his father and his uncle Worcester in these words:

> . . . yet time serves wherein you may redeem
> Your banished honours, and restore yourselves
> Into the good thoughts of the world again,
> Revenge the jeering and disdained contempt
> Of this proud king . . .　　　　　　　　　(I.iii. 180–184)

And a moment later, he says of himself in the famous speech:

> By heaven, methinks it were an easy leap,
> To pluck bright honour from the pale-faced moon . . . .
> So he that doth redeem her thence might wear
> Without corrival all her dignities:
> But out upon this half-faced fellowship!　　　(201–208)

With Hotspur commited to rebellion against the king, we have the three main forces of the play, as well as Hal himself, all resolved to redeem the time. The meaning of the phrase alters, of course, depending on who uses it; and it will have still another and larger meaning when the total action is complete. Already crown and field stand in clear opposition; Falstaff, linked to Hal rather than to the others, represents an unknown quantity so far; and Hal himself represents a variable, at least as to the time and nature of his commitment. If his resolve and realization are to become the focal point of the action, each of the forces must play its part in bringing about his reformation; and he, in turn, must pay the debt he "never promiséd" in such a way as to affect them all in redeeming the time.

—Hugh Dickinson, "The Reformation of Prince Hal,"
Shakespeare Quarterly 12, No. 1 (Winter 1961): 33–35

[Anthony La Branche is a professor of English at Loyola University's Lake Shore Campus. In this extract, La Branche contrasts the characters of Hal and Hotspur in *Henry IV, Part One*.]

When Henry remarks to Hal, in Act III, that as a young political aspirant, he "stole all courtesy from heaven", he is referring to the gracious practice of royal bowing, of "dressing one's actions in humility", a political gesture, not an ideal. Hal, amid the society of drawers at the Boar's Head, bemusedly treasures his title as "king of courtesy"—he knows among that company how to "sound the very base string of humility", as his father did before him. Hotspur, aroused by impending battle, twice uses the word *courtesy* in V. ii, each time alluding to the chivalric ideal of friendship among warriors. The play suggests contrasts more complex than these. Tillyard reminds us that Hal's gracefulness, his *sprezzatura,* or nonchalance, is symbolic of the new order of right acting and right governing, while Hotspur's notion of honor as military glory is antiquated. This formulates rather neatly the image each character holds up to us, but throughout the play we are also made aware of the practical advantages in Hal's graceful flexibility. Castiglione remarks that "the aim of the perfect Courtier . . . is to win for himself, by the means of the accomplishments ascribed to him . . . the favor and mind of the prince whom he serves that he may be able to tell him, and always will tell him, the truth about everything he needs to know." Courtesy is an instrument, the object of the instrument is influence, and the purpose of that instrument is virtue. Good and effective counsel, then, is the practical end of the courtier's art. Notably enough, it is not by his curiously original and modern "self-expression", which Tillyard admires, that Hal wins the confidence of his father, and of the realm, but by his adopting for the occasion in III. ii the same chivalric code through which Hotspus errs. But for Hal, in his interview with the King and thereafter, the code works, and effectively. The important difference between Hal and Hotspur lies in the public application, not in the terms of the code. Hal's story is one of assuming responsibilities, not of being educated into doing so; and his basic superiority to Hotspur lies in his natural growth into the new mode of applying virtue and into the new mode of governing. Hotspur possesses no inheritance, no cultural or political vision, into which he may grow. It is in the application that his virtue is patently inadequate.

The contrast which the out-of-date Hotspur presents to Hal, however, is not simply one of old to new, provincialism to gracefulness. On many counts Hal appears the exemplary antidote to Hotspur: he is flexible, not given to scorn of groups outside his social class, nor to detraction of his enemies, and at the end he takes upon himself that majesty which, in Elyot's words, consists in "honorable and sobre demeanure" and is "the fountaine of all excellent maners". Yet somehow, these differences do not add up to the sharp and obvious cleavage between Hal and Hotspur that commentators seek to draw; for the basic private virtues do not go out of date though their manifestations may. Behind our admiration of Hal's coming to perfect balance we retain the awareness that to be up-to-date is to be more effective, not necessarily more virtuous, in a private sense.

One curious and entertaining instance of Shakespeare's constant recognition of this discrepancy between the private and public faces of virtue occurs when Hotspur attacks Owen Glendower's show of courtesy in III. i. This scene is ordinarily valued for its fine portrayal of the rash Hotspur and his incidental satire of "metre ballad-mongers". It is odd that Hotspur and Glendower should take issue not only in matters of the tripartite division and Glendower's supernatural wizardry, but also in the matter of court manners. Hotspur is rude and cavilling, but he makes it clear that he has been antagonized by the sanctimonious pretensions of Glendower and the others. Likewise, it is the affectation of laborious versifiers that he hates, not culture as a whole, as his appreciation of the Welsh musicians testifies (III. i. 230). Glendower has asserted his allegiance to the Italianate ideal of the graceful courtier, fashioner of ditties, a "virtue that was never seen in you", close upon his supernatural sanction of the rebellious cause. Hotspur is repelled by both of these "outward shows".

> *Mortimer:* Fie, cousin Percy! how you cross my father!
> *Hotspur:* I cannot choose. Sometimes he angers me

> With telling me of the mouldwarp and the ant,
> Of the dreamer Merlin and his prophecies,
> And of a dragon and a finless fish,
> A clip-winged griffin and moulten raven,
> A couching lion and a ramping cat,
> And such a deal of skimble-skamble stuff
> As put me from my faith.   (III. i. 145ff.)

"Faith" in the cause or faith in what, we are not told. Hotspur is close to suggesting, however, that some notion of natural conduct is a motive of his resistance to Glendower's sanctimonious and graceful "appearances". When the politic Worcester takes him to task for losing men's hearts, he answers, "Well, I am school'd: good manners be your speed." And immediately, to spite these same shallow manners, he perversely insists that Lady Percy also enter the courtly competition and sing, or, if she will not, at least swear, like a lady, "a good mouth-filling oath".

The scene strikes us as deeply comic: Hotspur, the intolerant, the near-sighted, the self-deluded, attacks superstition, false religion, false reasoning, false manners, yet insists on forcing the Trent against nature. He is sensitive, it seems, to all falsely assumed codes save his own. But here is the crux, for Hotspur is not conscious that he, too, has adopted a code, and for all his absurdity one feels that Hotspur is acting according to his nature. Now this brings up the other side of the virtue of courtesy. Although both English and Italian writers admit that it is a basic and effective instrument in commanding respect and (especially for the English) in governing, neither will allow that courtesy can be pasted on from without, or assumed as a mere technique uninformed by a spirit. It issues from and gives expression of an inner light. For this reason the courtier must first be a whole man, and this is why we find ourselves at times in sympathy with Hotspur, against our saner senses, and why Hal, upon being reprimanded by his father for his waywardness and shame to the realm, must promise regeneration in these words: "I shall, hereafter, my thrice gracious lord, / Be more myself."

—Anthony La Branche, " 'If Thou Wert Sensible of Courtesy':
Private and Public Virtue in *Henry IV, Part One*," *Shakespeare
Quarterly* 17, No. 4 (Autumn 1966): 376–78

H. M. RICHMOND ON SHAKESPEARE'S POLITICS

[H. M. Richmond (b. 1932) is a professor of English and director of the Shakespeare program at the University of California at Berkeley. He has written studies of *Richard III* (1989) and *Henry VIII* (1994) as well as *Shakespeare's Sexual Comedy* (1971). In this extract from *Shakespeare's Political Plays* (1967), Richmond argues that Shakespeare's royalist politics are made explicit in his handling of the turbulent reign of Henry IV.]

Shakespeare usually identifies respect for the Crown as the lynch-pin of society—even when its powers are cavalierly misdirected by such a figure as Richard II—but nothing stresses this point much more than the sad spectacle of the kingdom of England as it appears under Bolingbroke, now King Henry IV. He is king by might rather than right for, even with Richard dead, there were closer direct heirs than the Lancastrian branch of the Plantagenets led by Henry. Henry shows from the opening lines of *Henry IV* that he is a master of that tactical skill whose lack was the major factor in Richard's initial loss of control. Henry's opening declamation is a masterpiece of calculation in the interests of preserving his all too precarious authority. Henry has the sense to see that, if he is to be identified adequately with the Crown, he must continually maintain the initiative, so that there is never time to raise the question of the legality of his succession. His proposal of a Crusade against the Moslems in the Holy Land is a stroke of political genius: the war will assert his authority, distract the more bellicose elements in English society, and suggest a proper piety in one who otherwise might be said to have stolen the Crown (alternatively, it might be held to be a fitting penance for a necessary but regrettable act).

There is, however, a further level of irony, for it soon becomes clear not only that the Crusade that Henry proposes has been rather promptly invalidated by the bad news of the Welsh rebellion that Westmoreland is forced to announce, but also that Henry from the start has scarcely expected to mount the expedition he so piously proposed. He therefore expresses no real surprise or distress at the breaking of his plans, saying only:

> It seems then that the tidings of this broil
> Brake off our business for the Holy Land. (l. i. 47–8)

In fact, it may even appear that Westmoreland is being manipulated as a herald of evil tidings, for he is now led on to reveal other gloomy news, from Scotland. In this disturbing atmosphere, Henry is able to stage a further reassuring announcement: the happy outcome of the Scottish campaign, which he presents personally in order to suggest his own authoritative intelligence about English affairs. This efficiency further appears in his order to have Hotspur return to London in order to explain his misconduct in withholding his prisoners from the king.

However, the impression of competent authority that the king in this manner plausibly sustains is not borne out by the facts with which he has to cope. Not only does he have to meet invasions from the west and the north, which involve his own shaky succession, but his lieutenants, such as Mortimer and Hotspur, are either incompetent or unpredictable. And more serious still, the whole future of the kingdom is darkened by the prospect of an even less sound succession to Henry than was his own to Richard. Hearing Hotspur's success, Henry is reminded of the sad prospect provided by his son and heir:

> Yea, there thou makest me sad and makest me sin
> In envy that my Lord Northumberland
> Should be the father to so blest a son,
> A son who is the theme of honour's tongue;
> Amongst a grove, the very straightest plant;
> Who is sweet Fortune's minion and her pride:
> Whilst I, by looking for the praise of him,
> See riot and dishonour stain the brow
> Of my young Harry. O that it could be proved
> That some night-tripping fairy had exchanged
> In cradle-clothes our children where they lay, . . . (l. i. 78–88)

The failure in Henry's handling of purely personal relationships is reflected in this impolitic speech, and his later coarse reproaches to his son illustrate the harsh terms that he imposes on those closest to him. It appears that he continues, as king, to force into opposition against him those very qualities of youthful spontaneity that were originally Richard's. Neither Hotspur nor Hal is able to live on friendly terms with him.

As the play develops, Shakespeare demonstrates how the dislocations engendered by Richard's indifference to matters of mere policy have developed and multiplied as the result of Henry's example, so that English society is becoming increasingly disorganized by greed from top to bottom. Not only do the Percys rebel; even the humble carriers on their way to London receive poor service in inns where the very staff themselves arrange plans for highway robbery of the guests. There was nothing visibly unnatural or monstrous about the kingdom of Richard II, but under Henry the evil genius of new England crystallizes in a Shakespearean figure as characteristic of the times as Richard III had been of the Wars of the Roses: Falstaff.

—H. M. Richmond, *Shakespeare's Political Plays* (New York: Random House, 1967), pp. 141–43

JAMES WINNY ON BOLINGBROKE AND HAL

[James Winny is the author of *Introduction to Chaucer* (1965) and *Chaucer's Dream Poems* (1973). In this extract from *The Player King* (1968), a study of Shakespeare's histories, Winny examines Bolingbroke's relationship with his son, Prince Hal.]

Because moral blindness prevents Bolingbroke from seeing himself in his apparently dissolute son, Hal's parentage is called into question. The uncertainty is taken up by Falstaff, who develops the theme comically during his royal performance in the tavern, and so echoes the doubts raised by Bolingbroke several scenes earlier:

> That thou art my son I have partly thy mother's words, partly
> my own opinion, but chiefly a villainous trick of thine eye,
> and a foolish hanging of thy nether lip, that doth warrant me.
> II. 4. 397–400

A heavily obvious pun in an earlier scene, where Falstaff talks about its being 'here apparent that thou art heir-apparent', touches on the same theme; and when Hal repudiates the suggestion that he should join in a robbery, Falstaff makes the issue a test of the Prince's legitimacy:

> Thou cam'st not of the blood royal, if thou darest not stand for
> ten shillings.   I. 2. 136f.

Here the joke has a satirical edge, for if Hal can prove his credentials by taking part in a highway robbery, that is because he has a master-thief as father; but the challenge helps to keep alive the question of Hal's parentage. The moral paradox argued by Falstaff, that 'the true prince may, for recreation sake, prove a false thief', involves the same issue and links princely authenticity with criminal habits, though Falstaff's proposal is impudently ambiguous. Beneath the simple meaning 'show himself to be a rascally cutpurse', his statement conceals a suggestion that Hal intends to expose, through his own seeming disrespect for law, the hidden falseness of the royal thief. Falstaff is unconsciously revealing part of the purpose of Hal's playing holidays.

The questioning of his identity concerns Hal through the suggestion that not he but Hotspur is the genuine heir-apparent; an idea which even Bolingbroke helps to encourage. Ignoring the historical fact that Hotspur was Hal's senior by twenty-three years, Shakespeare presents them as young men of the same age, whose political hostility is sharpened by a personal antagonism which finds expression on both sides in ridicule. Hotspur's disparaging reference to 'that same sword and buckler Prince of Wales' whom he considers poisoning with a pot of ale is repaid with interest in Hal's sardonic description of his rival, who nonchalantly 'kills me some six or seven dozen of Scots at breakfast'. They do not meet before their encounter at Shrewsbury, and nothing accounts for their mutual animosity; but both accept the assertion made by Hal before they fight:

> Two stars keep not their motion in one sphere,
> Nor can one England brook a double reign
> Of Harry Percy and the Prince of Wales.   V. 4. 64–66

Hal does not merely suggest that there is insufficient room for them both in the kingdom, but that Hotspur and he are bent upon filling a single role, and that one of them must be eliminated. The phrase, 'a double reign', carries its familiar suggestion of equivocal being, explained here by the physical similarity of the two young men who are rivals both for the succession and for the identity of authentic prince. Bolingbroke, who recognises that Hotspur enjoys 'no right, nor colour like to right', argues that none the less his energy and noble spirit give him a stronger claim to the throne than the Prince:

> He hath more worthy interest to the state
> Than thou the shadow of succession.   III. 2. 98f.

The remark is a direct challenge to Hal to prove his authenticity, and a partial explanation of the instinctive dislike which the Prince shows towards Hotspur. By standing out against the chorus of praise to which even his father subscribes, the Prince invites an assumption that he is envious of Hotspur, who usurps the place left vacant by Hal as the natural leader of chivalrous youth, and attracts general admiration by his valour and dash.

—James Winny, *The Player King: A Theme of Shakespeare's Histories* (London: Chatto & Windus, 1968), pp. 138–41

ROBERT ORNSTEIN ON THE STRUCTURE OF *HENRY IV, PART ONE*

[Robert Ornstein (b. 1925) is a professor of English at Western Reserve University and the author of *The Moral Vision of Jacobean Tragedy* (1960) and *Shakespeare's Comedies: From Roman Farce to Romantic Mystery* (1986). In this extract from his study of Shakespeare's history plays, *A Kingdom for a Stage* (1972), Ornstein discusses the structure and tone of *Henry IV, Part One*.]

After the deliberate formality of *Richard II,* the spontaneity of *Henry IV Part 1* seems all the more miraculous. It is as if the problem of dramatic structure, so carefully worked out in *Richard II,* suddenly ceased to exist for Shakespeare because his genius had repealed the laws of artistic gravity and discipline. The more we study *Henry IV,* the more we are impressed by the artfulness of its design: the parallelisms of its scenes, the echoings of motif and theme, and the juxtapositions and contrasts of character and attitude. Still, there is no sense of contrivance as the action unfolds, because the plot seems to be created moment by moment by the characters without the author's intervention. The tavern scenes are literally extempore; the clashes of personalities in the palace or in the rebels' councils have the immediacy and unpredictability of life. Thus, even though we know that the spontaneity of *Henry IV* is a virtuosic contrivance, the sleight of hand is so masterful that the artistic patterns seem marvelous coincidences, not continuing reminders of the author's shaping intelligence.

One pays a price, however, for the illusion of spontaneity, because casualness cannot be hurried or cut to measure. "Improvisation" must have scope to mirror the random quality of experience, the odd turns of conversation and mood. Either the plot must lengthen to include the holiday of the tavern scenes or the audience must settle for less of the serious matter of politics and history. Four-fifths as long as *Richard III, Henry IV Part 1* contains but a fraction of its Chronicle material; and its account of the past seems a trifle sketchy compared to the vast panorama of history that unfolds in each of the *Henry IV* plays. The Percy rebellion is all that we know of the early years of Henry's reign, and even that momentous political event remains until the last act in the background rather than the foreground of the plot. Before Shrewsbury, most of the drama of the uprising occurs offstage, not behind the scenes but rather between them, so that we catch only oblique reflections of the developing pattern of events as Hotspur reads a letter from a reluctant ally or as reports of the rebellion reach the tavern. Such important figures as Northumberland, Mortimer, and Glendower appear only once and then not in scenes that reveal them as political leaders. We see how passionately Mortimer loves his Welsh wife and how Glendower's sorcery irritates Hotspur, but we do not know the political motives which keep Mortimer and Glendower from fighting by Hotspur's side at Shrewsbury.

I do not mean to suggest that the portrayal of history in *Part 1* is meager or perplexing. On the contrary, there is a greater depth of insight into political motives and relationships in *Part 1* than in the earlier History Plays, and there is a more inclusive view of the drama of politics than before, not despite the presence of the tavern scenes but because of them. It is easier, however, to appreciate Falstaff than to explain how the comic scenes join with the "serious action" of the play to make up a larger artistic whole. When we see a fine performance of *Part 1,* we have no doubt of the unity of its plot and its conception; when we try to analyze this unity, it proves ineffable. Either we find ourselves documenting subtle parallels and elusive echoes that no audience would apprehend, or we create the impression that the play has a "double" rather than a single plot which creates one dramatic world in the tavern scenes, another in those of the palace. We can, of course, hold the plot together by making the tavern scenes nothing more than a conventional setting for the drama of Hal's escape from the temptation to vanity and riot. But to conventionalize the tavern scenes, we must close our eyes to all that is subversive of homiletic earnestness in the dialogue and play-acting in the Boar's Head, and if we ignore the subversive charm and ironic perspective of the comic scenes, we cannot then justify their disproportionate share of the dramatic action. Who, moreover, can take seriously the "Morality drama" of the tavern scenes in which the prodigal is not very prodigal or susceptible to temptation, but the audience is so easily enchanted by the figure of Riot that only the warnings of scholarship guard it from seduction?

It is one thing to speak of the "dramatic balance" of *Henry IV, Part 1,* as do Brooks and Heilman, who see it a "view which scants nothing, which covers up nothing, and which takes into account in making its affirmations the most searching criticism of that which is affirmed." It is another thing to dwell on the ironic poise, tensions, ambivalences, and ambiguities of Shakespeare's art as if there were an irreducible parallax in his vision of reality. The amplitude of Shakespearean drama does not depend upon the presence of dialectical oppositions, for the comprehensiveness and "balance" of his vision is evident in every scene, in every line of his plays. It is very doubtful, for example, that Hal's caricaturing of Hotspur in the tavern really qualifies an audience's perception of Percy; and it is even more doubtful that this mockery is required to balance or correct an audience's admiration for Hotspur's youthful heroism. The scenes of Hotspur with his family, his wife, and his allies tell all we need to know about the egotism of his motives and the rashness of his enthusiasm. Conversely, we do not need the scenes of Hotspur to recognize that the saturnalia of the Boar's Head is not an ideal representation of the good cheer and fellowship, because Hal is restless at times and bored, and always condescending to his companions, whom he promises to cast off.

—Robert Ornstein, *A Kingdom for a Stage: The Achievement of Shakespeare's History Plays* (Cambridge, MA: Harvard University Press, 1972), pp. 125–27

ROY BATTENHOUSE ON FALSTAFF'S CHRISTIAN NATURE

[Roy Battenhouse (b. 1912), formerly a professor of English at Indiana University, is the author of *A Companion to the Study of St. Augustine* (1955) and *Shakespearean Tragedy: Its Art and Its Christian Premises* (1969). In this extract, Battenhouse explores the assertions of other scholars that Falstaff has a truly Christian nature.]

It was suggested by Lord Fitz Roy Raglan, in 1936, that "Shakespeare had in the back of his mind the idea that Falstaff was a holy man." And W. H. Auden, more recently, has argued in cryptic fashion that Falstaff, while overtly a Lord of Misrule, is nevertheless at heart "a comic symbol for the supernatural order of charity." By other scholars there has been an understandable reluctance to pick up or probe this possibility. For it fits not at all with Prince Hal's view when banishing Falstaff as a profane fool and abominable misleader. And no doubt few of today's playgoers think of imputing charity to a Falstaff whose prankish chicanery and braggadocio seem to make him the very image of traditional vice, garnished at one time or other with all Seven Deadlies. Yet may not the fulsome display of reprobation be more mask than inner man? One of Auden's most tantalizing points is to remind us that the Sermon on the Mount enjoins Christians to show charity through a secret almsgiving not trumpeted, and to fast while not appearing unto men to fast. Could this be a clue to the enigma of Falstaff's character? Perhaps so, I think, provided we put beside it Lord Raglan's intuition that Falstaff's vocation, in the public world, is that of court fool and soothsayer. Such a double hypothesis, in any case, seems to me to warrant a trying out and testing. For it could mean that while as "allowed fool" Falstaff is shamming vices and enacting parodies, his inner intent is a charitable almsgiving of brotherly self-humiliation and fatherly truth-telling.

It could mean, further, that the relation of Falstaff to the Lollard martyr Oldcastle, a matter that scholars have puzzled over since Shakespeare juggled their names, is a relation of paradoxical affinity. For on the one hand, as the play's Epilogue tells us, Falstaff is not the man Oldcastle (a solemn martyr for views unconventional in his times); yet is not Falstaff, though comic, also a nobleman whose seeming affronts to officialdom make him a martyr? The mode of witnessing is of course different. A clown, if and while Christian at heart, must mask his piety under absurd posturings and perhaps facial leers. His office is to offer spectacle of himself in the lineaments of folly, as a mirror to the great of their own imperfections. But such a vocation runs the risk of banishment at the hands of princes whose morals are those of worldly self-advantage and political expediency. By such princes the Fool's mirror is rejected as disreputably profane, even when marginally it reflects Christian premises.

In Shakespeare's *Henry IV* we can find, I think, much evidence for this interpretation of Falstaff's fate and of the enigma of his role. Let us listen, for instance, to Falstaff's last words to

Henry. There are three of them: "God save thy Grace, King Hal, my royal Hal!"; "God save thee, my sweet boy!"; and third (here placing Hal as an earthly god, but not God), "My King! My Jove! I speak to thee my heart." Each of these last words is an impeccably Christian prayer or plea, and I see no reason to suppose any of them ungenuine. A Jovian king deserves a jovial welcome, whether his visit be to some tavern as an aproned prentice or, as now, to public view in his royal robes. But since "royal Hal" is after all less than God, is it not appropriate to contextualize his welcome by invoking God's grace for the saving of the sweet boy within the official personage? Alas, for thus speaking his heart Falstaff is pilloried. He is berated as a "vain" man, told to fall to his knees in repentance, and warned not to expect "advancement" until he reforms. Is our martyr wholly surprised? To the Shallows of this world he ascribes the king's ungraciousness to what Hal must "seem" in public, thus charitably covering Hal's fault. But surely Falstaff has long anticipated that his rejection would come to pass. On his very first appearance in Part 1 he had said: "God save thy Grace—Majesty I should say, for *grace* thou wilt have none." This prophecy has been fulfilled. The prince whom Falstaff has labored to bring to knowledge of self has proved to be instead a Pontius Pilate, a graceless judge who has toyed with truth without staying for an answer. And the location, ironically, is a place near Westminster and its "Jerusalem" aura.

As compared with Oldcastle's martyrdom, Falstaff's has been even more humiliating. But is this not because his method of witnessing is more secret, more conditioned by the ancient folk wisdom of the Christian centuries? Recall, in this connection, three of St. Paul's guidelines for being a witness to the gospel mystery:

> God hathe chosen the foolish things of the world to confounde the wise. . . . For the wisdome of this world is foolishness with God. (I Cor. i.27, iii.19. All citations Geneva)

> We approve ourselves . . . by honour and dishonour, by evil reporte & good reporte, as deceivers, and yet true. (II Cor. vi.8)

> For we wrestle not against flesh and blood, but against . . . the worldlie governours, the princes of the darkness of this world, against spiritual wickedness, which are in the hie places. (Eph. vi.12)

These passages I think crucial for any insight into Falstaff. The fat knight has a "gravity" quite interior to his physical poundage: he lards the earth not merely with his sweat, but covertly with a Christian spirit as wise as serpents and as harmless as doves.

—Roy Battenhouse, "Falstaff as Parodist and Perhaps Holy Fool," *PLMA* 90, No. 1 (January 1975): 32–33

PETER SACCIO ON THE HISTORICAL BASIS OF *HENRY IV, PART ONE*

[Peter Saccio, a professor of English at Dartmouth College, has written *The Court Comedies of John Lyly* (1969) and *Shakespeare's English Kings* (1977), from which the following extract is taken. Here, Saccio examines the historical basis of *Henry IV, Part One,* arguing that history provided Shakespeare with rich and dramatic material.]

The reign of Henry IV came to Shakespeare's hand already possessed of a dramatic shape, a perceived pattern of historical cause and effect. In 1399, at about the age of thirty-three, Henry of Lancaster usurped the crown of his first cousin Richard II, retaining it until his own death of natural causes in 1413. Shakespeare's Henry, on his deathbed, attributes all the troubles of his reign to having "snatched" the crown. Henry's overthrow of Richard had implicitly invited others, when they became discontented with his rule, to attempt another disposition. Shakespeare's king exaggerates slightly: the last five years of Henry's reign were in fact free of major domestic upheaval. For the first eight years or so, however, he may have felt like the captain of an undermanned and badly caulked ship, plugging leaks that refused to stay plugged and continually having to move the pumps about. Wales was in revolt every summer from 1400 to 1408. During the same period a variety of English rebels beset him as well, hatching minor plots from time to time and causing major crises in 1403 and 1405. Until 1409, the best efforts of Henry himself and of his eldest son (whom I, to avoid confusion, will call by his Shakespearean nickname Hal) were devoted to keeping the house of Lancaster on the throne it had seized.

Henry IV was born Henry of Bolingbroke, only surviving son of the first marriage of John of Gaunt duke of Lancaster, who was in turn the third surviving son of Edward III. By his early thirties he had acquired a distinguished international reputation. He was famous as a jouster in tournaments; he had become an experienced campaigner while on crusade in Lithuania; he was noted for courtesy and generosity in the European courts that he had visited when returning from a pilgrimage to the Holy Land. He was energetic, learned, pious in an orthodox way, and popular among his own people. He was also a widower and the father of four sons. From time to time he played a significant role in English politics.

Since the circumstances of Bolingbroke's usurpation provide some of the issues over which the characters of *Henry IV* wrangle, they must be related briefly here. In 1398, as readers of the previous chapter will recall, mutual accusations of treason brought Bolingbroke and Thomas Mowbray duke of Norfolk to the point of trial by combat. The duel, however, never took place. King Richard, presiding over the ceremony, threw down his staff of office to interrupt the proceedings, and, after consultation with his council, exiled both men. Early in the following year, when Bolingbroke's father died, Richard seized the Lancastrian estates. Bolingbroke thereupon broke exile, returning from France in July to regain his inheritance. Landing in the north, he was joined by various powerful noblemen who volunteered their assistance in the recovery of his rights and the reform of Richard's erratic behavior and financially exacting government. He proceeded to secure the capitulation of Richard's officials and to execute some who were held particularly responsible for misleading the king (the so-called caterpillars of the commonwealth). Richard himself, meanwhile, was in Ireland, attempting to crush rebellion there, and thus found himself badly placed to deal with the threat of Bolingbroke. He was, moreover, held there for some time by contrary winds and poor communications. Upon his return to Wales, his mismanagement of his troops, the treachery of some of his supporters, and the stratagems of Bolingbroke's friends resulted in his capture. Although Bolingbroke originally appeared to be seeking only the duchy of Lancaster, the unpopularity and collapse of the king allowed him to seize the throne of England as well. Richard was deposed and Henry crowned. After certain earls loyal to Richard attempted to restore him in January 1400, Richard himself died a mysterious death in prison. It was widely thought that he was murdered on Henry's orders, or at least by Henry's friend on his behalf.

> —Peter Saccio, *Shakespeare's English Kings: History, Chronicle, and Drama* (New York: Oxford University Press, 1977), pp. 37–39

ROBERT N. WATSON ON KING HENRY'S GUILT AND HAL'S INCORRIGIBILITY

[Robert N. Watson (b. 1953), a professor of English at Harvard University, is the author of *Shakespeare and the Hazards of Ambition* (1984), from which the following extract is taken. Here, Watson asserts that King Henry sees a divine justice in Hal's misbehavior—a punishment for his own usurpation of the throne.]

Act three, scene two, of 1 *Henry IV* begins with Henry's interpreting Hal's misbehavior as a divine punishment for his own misdeeds. Though Henry, as usual, pretends to be slightly uncertain what his own crime might have been, a son's rebellious refusal to rise to the level of his royal blood would be an entirely appropriate rebuke to his father's insistence on rising to claim that royal heritage. The psychoanalytic maxim that the bad son has bad sons, and the physical maxim that what goes up must come down, both work to subvert Henry's hopes for a royal heir:

> I know not whether God will have it so
> For some displeasing service I have done,
> That in his secret doom, out of my blood,
> He'll breed revengement and a scourge for me;

> But thou dost in thy passages of life
> Make me believe that thou art only mark'd
> For the hot vengeance, and the rod of heaven,
> To punish my mistreadings. Tell me else,
> Could such inordinate and low desires,
> Such poor, such bare, such lewd, such mean attempts,
> Such barren pleasures, rude society,
> As thou art match'd withal and grafted to,
> Accompany the greatness of thy blood,
> And hold their level with thy princely heart? (3.2.4–17)

This insistence on blood finding its own level may be Henry's effort to bluster away the fact that "his blood was poor" until he stepped "a little higher than his vow" and usurped Richard's throne (4.3.75–76). Hal's "affections" may indeed "hold a wing / Quite from the flight of all thy ancestors," making him "almost an alien to the hearts / Of all the court and princes of my blood" (3.2.29–35), but Henry is also on an errant flight from his hereditary place. The system rights itself from within: in the very act of being a punitively bad son to Henry, Hal is said to resemble Richard, to stand "in that very line" of the man whose right it was to place his likeness on the throne (3.2.85–94).

As Henry becomes caught up in the excitement of scolding his son, his language reveals a recognition that this throne is actually founded on such externalities as costume rather than such internalities as blood. He boasts of clothing himself in the simulation of an inward virtue, and of maintaining his person as if it were a borrowed garment: he won the people's affection when he "dress'd myself in such humility / That I did pluck allegiance from men's hearts," yet retained their respect by keeping "my person fresh and new, / My presence like a robe pontifical . . ." (3.2.51–56). Marvell's warning to Cromwell in the "Horation Ode" that "The same arts that did gain / A power must it maintain" (lines 119–20) seems applicable to Henry here: he discovers that the kingship gained by replacing a natural identity with an artificial one, replacing a person with a garment, can only be maintained by his remaining a polished costume rather than an authentic human being.

The redefinition of kingship implicit in Henry's usurpation is inextricably linked to a redefinition of identity, and one result is that not only Hal, but Sir Walter Blunt, and even Jack Falstaff, can play the role of King Henry IV with some success (2.4, 5.3). If Hal is what his father here calls him abusively, "the shadow of succession," there is good reason for it (3.2.99). Even Hal's promise that he "shall hereafter . . . / Be more myself" (3.2.93) has ironic overtones as a response to his father's criticisms, since Henry has just finished arguing that he won the throne by retaining an artificial self, or at least an artificial distance from himself. Whether it is Hal's irony or Shakespeare's, Henry's effort to define a true heir is trapped in a contradiction of his own making.

> —Robert N. Watson, *Shakespeare and the Hazards of Ambition*
> (Cambridge, MA: Harvard University Press, 1984), pp. 55–56

GRAHAM HOLDERNESS ON FALSTAFF AS A POLITICAL AND MORAL FOIL TO THE KING

[Graham Holderness, dean of cultural and historical studies at the University of Hertfordshire, England, has written *Shakespeare's Myth* (1988), *Shakespeare out of Court: Dramatizations of Court Society* (1990), and *The Politics of Theatre and Drama* (1992). In this extract from *Shakespeare's History* (1985), Holderness sees Falstaff as a foil to the conventions of the English sovereign.]

It is commonplace that the figure of Falstaff, or the 'world' that figure inhabits or creates, constitutes some kind of internal *opposition* to the ethical conventions, political priorities and structures of authority and power embodied in the sovereign hegemony of king, prince and court: the state. Falstaff is at the centre of a popular comic history, located within the deterministic framework of the chronicle-history play, which challenges and subverts the imperatives of necessitarian historiography; and it is important to stress that the chronicle-history frame is qualified and criticised, not simply by the free play of

Shakespeare's 'wonderful' intelligence on the underlying issues, but by a confrontation of different dramatic discourses within the drama a confrontation which brings into play genuinely historical tensions and contradictions, drawn both from Shakespeare's own time and from the reconstructed time of the historical past.

The kind of 'opposition' represented by Falstaff is often compared with the other oppositional tendencies which challenge the state in these plays: Falstaff's moral rebelliousness and illegality are seen as analogous to those forces of political subversion—the rebellion of the Percies and the Archbishop of York's conspiracy—which shake the stability of the Lancastrian dynasty. But though moral riotousness and political opposition are often arbitrarily connected by hostile propaganda, a state which ruthlessly suppresses the latter often finds space for the former—regarded perhaps as the legitimate exercise of freedom guaranteed to a a despotic ruling class by the 'stability' of its government (e.g. the court of the Stuarts). It has been recognised that the revelry and satire of Falstaff constitute kinds of social practice which were afforded a legitimate space in medieval culture. Medieval European hierarchies, secular and ecclesiastical, sought to preserve the rigidity of their social relations, to control and incorporate internal tensions and oppositions, by allowing, at fixed times, temporary suspensions of rule, order and precedence: festive holidays in which moral freedom and opposition to political authority, the flouting of moral conventions and the inversion of ordinary social structures, were allowed to flourish. These periods of temporary suspension were closely analogous to, possibly related back to, religious practices of antiquity:

> Many peoples have been used to observe an annual period of licence, when the customary restraints of law and morality are thrown aside, when the whole population give themselves up to extravagant mirth and jollity, and when the darker passions find a vent which would never be allowed them in the more staid and sober course of ordinary life. Such outbursts of the pent-up forces of human nature, too often degenerating into wild orgies of lust and crime, occur most commonly at the end of the year, are frequently associated . . . with one or other of the agricultural seasons, especially with the time of sowing or of harvest. ⟨Sir James George Frazer, *The Golden Bough*⟩

Dance, song, feasting, moral freedom, were a natural element of most pre-Christian European religions, and were sternly condemned as unchristian, immoral licence by zealous and reforming Christian clerics, from the early Church fathers (who attacked the Roman Saturnalia) to the sixteenth-century Puritans. More generally they were modified, and incorporated into Christian observance (in the same way as the more prudent and discerning Christian missionaries tried to *adapt* rather than supplant the beliefs of those they wished to convert), so that the pagan fertility myths of the Mummers' Play became a Christmas or Springtime celebration. Such social practices were far from being simply a period of release, with bouts of drinking and lust and frenzied dancing: they were often characterised by a specific ritual shape, involving the suspension of ordinary structures of authority. The Roman Saturnalia reveals a clear ritual structure within the general surrender to appetite and passion: within it social relationships were not merely suspended but *inverted*:

> Now of all these periods of license the one which is best known and which in modern languages has given its name to the rest, is the Saturnalia . . . no feature of the festival is more remarkable, nothing in it seems to have struck the ancients themselves more than the licence granted to slaves at this time. The distinction between the free and servile classes was temporarily abolished. The slave might rail at his master, intoxicate himself like his betters, sit down at table with them, and not even a word of reproof would be administered to him for conduct which at any other season might have been punished with stripes, imprisonment, or death. Nay, more, masters actually changed places with their slaves and waited on them at table; and not till the serf had done eating and drinking was the board cleared and dinner set for his master. ⟨Frazer⟩

The custom was called the saturnalian because it purported to be a temporary imitation of the 'Golden Age' society of peace, fertility, freedom and common wealth, without private property or slavery presided over by the God Saturn: 'The Saturnalia passed for nothing more or less than a temporary revival of restoration of the reign of that merry monarch'. The nostalgic sentimentalism of Roman patricians and the utopian longings of their slaves met on the common ground of saturnalian revelry and ritual: a clear acknowledgment that such a society must have been preferable to the present order, co-existed with a more pragmatic sense of the essentially limited nature of human ideals and aspirations, a sad recognition that 'order' (i.e. the contemporary state) can be suspended, but never, in practice, abolished or transformed. So the Saturnalia, and the associated rituals of medieval Europe, were

> . . . an interregnum during which the customary restraints of law and morality are suspended and the ordinary rulers abdicate their authority in favour of a temporary regent, a sort of puppet king, who bears a more or less indefinite, capricious and precarious sway over a community given up for a time to riot, turbulence and disorder. ⟨Frazer⟩

Similar customs are visible in later English folk-ceremonies by which the rural people celebrated spring or summer: Festivities in praise of fertility would involve the election of a mock ruler— a 'May King', a 'Summer Lord', a 'Mock Mayor'—or a King and Queen whose mock marriage would seem to symbolise some ancient myth of fertility. Such festivities, it is suspected, would probably include the exercise of practical fertility among the celebrants: 'It may be taken for granted that the summer festivals knew from the beginning that element of sexual licence which fourteen centuries of Christianity have not wholly been able to banish'. ⟨E. K. Chambers, *The Mediaeval Stage*⟩

—Graham Holderness, *Shakespeare's History* (New York: St. Martin's Press, 1985), pp. 79–82

PAUL N. SIEGEL ON CLASS DISTINCTIONS IN *HENRY IV,* PART ONE

[Paul N. Siegel (b. 1916) is a former professor of English at Long Island University in Brooklyn, New York. He has written voluminously on Shakespeare, including such books as *Shakespearean Tragedy and the Elizabethan Compromise* (1957) and *Shakespeare in His Time and Ours* (1968). In this extract from his Marxist interpretation of Shakespeare, Siegel examines

63

the social and economic differences between Hotspur and Hal.]

The contrast in Tudor times between the old feudalistic aristocracy and the new aristocracy is best exemplified by the opposition between Hotspur and Hal. To repeat partially what I have said elsewhere,

> "Hotspur is a figure representative of the Elizabethan period as well as of the feudal past . . . . Hotspur's concept of honor (the most dedicated of whom were members of the old aristocracy in Elizabeth's court) who argued, according to Bryskett, that '. . . a man for cause of honour may arm himself against his country.' Full of the sense of his family's 'nobility and power,' he feels that Henry has disgraced it and seeks to avenge the family honor, urging his father and uncle to 'redeem/your banished honors' and 'revenge the jeering and disdained contempt/ Of this proud king' (I, iii, 170–82). . . . Hotspur has the old feudal contempt of the humanistic virtues of the gentleman . . . [He] is not the man for what he calls 'mincing poetry' (III, i, 34). Hunting and war are his pursuits . . . . In killing Hotspur, Hal, who has 'a truant been to chivalry,' (V,i,94) takes over Hotspur's chivalric virtues, but he purges them of their accompanying faults. He is not concerned, as is Hotspur, who could brook no "corrival," (I, iii, 205) with a reputation of preeminent valor, but rather concerned with the honor that comes from doing public service, an honor that in his speech before Agincourt he calls upon the commonest soldier to share with him."

The bourgeoisie, whom Hotspur regards with contempt (3.1.251–54), is an intermittently perceived force throughout the plays. The significance of its support of Bolingbroke has already been examined. To Green's statement that the king's favorites are hated by those who "love not the King," Bagot replies (2.2 128–130), "And that is the wavering commons, for their love / Lies in their purses, and whoso empties them / By so much fills their hearts with deadly hate." The "wavering commons" often is decisive, at least for the moment, in the struggle of the rival houses. "Trust me, my lord," says Warwick, the "kingmaker" (3 Henry VI, 4.2 1–2), after having switched from Edward IV to Henry VI, "all hitherto goes well; / The common people by numbers swarm to us."

The bourgeoisie is primarily concerned with two things: the relief from taxes of which Bagot speaks and the maintenance of a strong central government that would put down disorders and protect the flow of trade. The Bishop of Winchester, the great uncle of the king, vying with Humphrey of Gloucester, uncle of the King and Protector of the realm, seeks to incite the Lord Mayor of London against him by saying (*1 Henry VI,* 1.3.62–64), "Here's Gloucester, a foe to citizens, / One that still motions war and never peace, / O'ercharging your free purses with large fines." The Lord Mayor's attitude toward these mighty ones, whose retainers have engaged in an altercation that has raised an uproar, is one of a "plague on both your houses": "Fie, lords! that you, being supreme magistrates,/ Thus contumeliously should break the peace!" (57–58). He proclaims that all those who have engaged in this disturbance "against God's peace and the king's" (75) must disperse immediately and henceforth not wear weapons, threatening to call out the apprentices from their shops to assist the city officers if the combatants do not leave the scene. The strength of the bourgeoisie here apparent is even more clearly seen in the fact that Richard III feels that he needs the support of the Lord Mayor and the leading citizens, the commercial oligarchy of London, before he can be crowned king.

Shakespeare, then does more than show the changing relationship between monarchy, aristocracy, and bourgeoisie and the evolution of each in the historical period he is depicting. He shows the changes in his own time and even foreshadows the time when the bourgeoisie and its allies will overthrow a Stuart king.

—Paul N. Siegel, *Shakespeare's English and Roman History Plays: A Marxist Approach* (Rutherford, NJ: Fairleigh Dickinson University Press, 1986), pp. 76–77

PAUL M. CUBETA ON FALSTAFF'S CONVENIENT DEATHS

[Paul M. Cubeta (b. 1925), is College Professor of Humanities and director of the Bread Loaf School of English at Middlebury College. He has edited

Twentieth Century Interpretations of Richard II (1971). In this extract, Cubeta explores the many deaths and resurrections of Falstaff throughout the Henriad.]

Once the historical myths and dramatic concerns of *The Henriad* served by Falstaff's comic vision have been resolved by his legendary repudiation, Falstaff the character can no longer exist: "Reply not to me with a foolborn jest" (Shakespeare, *2H4* V.v.55). On that command to silence, the newly crowned king has destroyed his fool and jester. Falstaff could undergo a mock-magical death and resurrection at the end of *1 Henry IV*, and he essentially "dies of a sweat" at the end of *2 Henry IV*, when he races recklessly to Westminster Abbey "to stand stain'd with travel, and sweating with desire to see" Hal newly crowned (V.v.24–25). But Falstaff the man cannot be dismissed or lie forgotten in Fleet Prison, abandoned by king and playwright. The Shakespearean investment in the saving grace of that comic spirit in his Lancastrian world has been too great. And so in *Henry V* he redeems Epilogue's promise in *2 Henry IV* to continue the story "with Sir John in it" (Epi., 28) with a vividly realized, yet non-existent death scene, both comic and pathetic, private and demonstrated, dedicated to the spirit of Falstaff the man.

Never allowed securely to grasp this protean giant even when his comic imagination and ironic vision die, the audience participated in the immediacy and intensity of the deathbed scene but not by observing those who stand at Falstaff's bedside. Simultaneously the audience is kept at double distance from the mystery of Falstaff's dying thoughts. Instead of sentimental farewell in the cold, pragmatic Lancastrian world, Shakespeare seeks instead a resolution in which tragedy and comedy, doubt and belief, clarity and confusion are bound in a manner historically appropriate, morally satisfying, and psychologically dazzling. The theatrical gamble of creating a character by not creating him, of giving him life by destroying him yields the most memorable scene of the play.

To achieve the dense texture of this recollected deathbed scene, Shakespeare does not turn to his usual source for things even vaguely Falstaffian in *The Henriad*—*The Famous Victories of Henry V* (1598). In the life of Falstaff, Shakespeare has embodied rituals, folk tales, conventions, festivals as familiar to an Elizabethan audience as those he may now be suggestively recalling in the medieval and Renaissance tradition of *ars moriendi,* or the art of dying. To design a coherent structure and meaning to Falstaff's dying moments of introspection and memory, which appear as merely broken, delirious fragments, Shakespeare may also give Falstaff the occasion to attempt a private meditation on his life in the manner of a Renaissance meditation for Wednesday night.

Reported in an intensely moving yet uncertain retelling, Falstaff's mode of dying is as mysterious and as hauntingly perplexing as any circumstance in his life. The only words directly attributed to him, the great inventor of language, are "God, God, God!" (*H5* II.iii.19). But what this punster, this parodist and unparalleled player with the rhythms of spoken language, means or what tone the repetitions are spoken in is not ours to hear. The challenger of the moral, social, political, and religious values on which civilization rests dies with a word, the Word, on which pun cannot prevail. Like his heart, which Pistol avers, was "fracted and corroborate" (II.i.124), the scene recollecting Falstaff's death is a kind of transitory memorial moment, broken, unfocused, contradictory, unchronological and impossible to recreate for even their listeners by his bedside mourners, who are then about to be swept up into events in France and propelled to their own deaths.

—Paul M. Cubeta, "Falstaff and the Art of Dying," *Studies in English Literature 1500–1900* 27, No. 2 (Spring 1987): 197–98

ALEXANDER LEGGATT ON DECEPTION IN *HENRY IV, PART ONE*

[Alexander Leggatt (b. 1940), a professor of English at the University of Toronto, is the author of *Shakespeare's Political Drama: The History Plays and the Roman Plays* (1988), from which the following extract is taken. Here, Leggatt comments on

Shakespeare's use of deception in *Henry IV, Part One,*
with the result that nothing in the play is as it seems.]

The rebels are concerned with appearances, no less than the
King and his son, and this concern replaces the simpler agres-
siveness that drove the rebels of *Henry VI.* When Hotspur
promises his colleagues,

> yet time serves wherein you may redeem
> Your banish'd honours, and restore yourselves
> Into the good thoughts of the world again.   (Pt 1, I. iii. 178–80)

we catch echoes from the end of the previous scene, Hal's
soliloquy announcing his strategy. Hotspur even uses two of
Hal's key words 'redeem' and 'time' (cf. I. ii. 212). The rebels'
calculations before Shrewsbury include considerations of reputation: Worcester thinks Northumberland's absence will make
the rebellion look bad; Hotspur argues it will make it look better, showing they can carry on without his help. The anxiety
behind these calculations shows that the world of appearances
demands tricky manoeuvring; Hotspur says he would praise
Douglas properly 'If speaking truth / In this fine age were not
thought flattery' (IV. i. 1–2). Besides kingship, there are other
kinds of coinage that can be debased. Moreover, the characters' attempts to master appearances are complicated by the
fact that they are not in a single world where everyone speaks
the same language, but in a fragmented one. This is no longer
the tight stage community of *Richard II,* in which all eyes could
be fixed on one figure; there, no one, down to the meanest
gardener or groom, was excluded from the circle of attention
centred on Richard. The world of *Henry IV,* on the other hand,
is widely dispersed and richly varied. When Sir Walter Blunt
appears in the first scene 'Stain'd with the variation of each soil
/ Betwixt that Holmedon and this seat of ours' (I.i. 64–5), the
lines evoke the physical variety of the land, and anticipate the
play's treatment of other kinds of variety. No single image can
stand, as did the sea-walled garden of the earlier play, for the
entire nation. Similarly, when Mortimer complains, 'My wife
can speak no English, I no Welsh' (III.i.187), this is a simple
reflection of a general problem; in other ways, as we shall see,
characters in *Henry IV* do not speak each other's languages.

(Shakespeare is not just making a cheap joke about political marriages here; through the barrier imposed by language we see the affection of a couple who really wish they *could* speak to each other.)

Misinformation is a recurring motif. Part 2 opens under the aegis of the presenter Rumour with a totally garbled version of the ending of the previous play. Characters are always complaining of being misunderstood or misquoted. In the controversy over whatever Hotspur denied the King his prisoners, Northumberland claims they 'Were . . . not with such strength deny'd / As is deliver'd to your Majesty' (Pt 1, I. iii. 24–5), while Hotspur flatly declares, 'My liege, I did deny no prisoners' (I.iii.28), only to admit later that he cannot remember what he said (I. iii. 51–2). Hal blames his troubles with his father on 'many tales devis'd . . . By smiling pickthanks, and base newsmongers' (III. ii 23–5), and having rescued him at Shrewsbury declares, 'O God, they did me too much injury / That ever said I hearken'd for your death' (V. iv. 50–1). Worcester is wary of any accommodation with the King, because 'Look how we can, or sad or merrily, / Interpretation will misquote our looks' (V. ii. 12–13). By the time John of Lancaster assures the rebels at Gaultree, 'My father's purposes have been mistook' (Pt 2, IV. ii 56), the complaint has become a regular part of political discourse, and they believe it.

This is a world, then, in which appearances matter, and are not to be trusted. At its centre is the counterfeit king who is the only king England has. He is no longer the quietly expert politician of *Richard II*. At the opening of Part 1 he appears surrounded with his nobles, a familiar image of power and authority, but first words are 'So shaken as we are, so wan with care' (Pt 1, I. i. 1). He goes on to promise domestic peace and harmony:

> No more the thirsty entrance of this soil
> Shall daub her lips with her own children's blood,
> No more shall trenching war channel her fields,
> Nor bruise her flow'rets with the armed hoofs
> Or hostile paces.   (Pt 1, I. i. 5–9)

He sounds like Richmond at the end of *Richard III*; but the promises are all negative, and the placing of the speech at the beginning of the play makes it vulnerable. Plays do not *begin* with reconciliation and harmony; the expectations built into the dramatic form itself sabotage Henry's vision. Richard of Gloucester also began his play announcing peace, but his announcement was frankly ironic, and he was in control of the irony as Henry is not. Elsewhere Henry shows executive firmness and strength of will. But the tact he demonstrated in dealing with the York family in *Richard II* has deserted him, or he no longer bothers to exercise it, in dealing with the Percies. He loses his temper with Worcester and orders him out, cutting off Northumberland in midsentence as he does so (I. iii. 10–21). When Blunt proposes a reconciliation, Henry will have none of it; he wants, and gets, a confrontation (I. iii. 69–91). This may be sound strategy in the long run, but the initial impression is of a man whose nerves are on edge. He has also a curious capacity for seeing the bad side even of good news. Told that Hotspur has won a victory on his behalf, he reflects gloomily on the contrast between Hotspur and his son (I. i. 77–85). This deepens in Part 2 into a terrible pessimism, a belief that it is better not to be born at all. If one could 'read the book of fate, / And see the revolution of the times' (Pt 2, III. I. 45–6), then

> The happiest youth, viewing his progress through,
> What perils past, what crosses to ensue,
> Would shut the book and sit him down and die.
>
> (Pt 2, III. i. 54–6)

Yet his torments are different from those of Richard III on the eve of Bosworth. Richard suffered a sharp and specific guilt; Henry, a deep but curiously unfocused *malaise*. Richard is haunted by his victims and tormented by his deeds; Henry is denied, or denies himself, such moral clarity. If he feels guilty he does not at at this point say so.

For one thing—and this reflects the more realistic idiom of this play—Henry does not sense around him the supernatural framework that Richard sees so clearly. He recalls Richard II's prophecy that Northumberland would betray him, but seems to accept Warwick's analysis of it. Richard, like Henry VI, has turned out to be a true prophet. But, while Henry's accuracy can be attributed only to supernatural inspiration, Richard's (Warwick argues) was simply an intelligent observation of the principles of political behaviour; anyone who studies the past carefully can make a fair stab at predicting the future (Pt 2, III. i. 80–92). In place of Richard III's flamboyant defiance of his conscience, we hear Henry's quiet 'Are these things then necessities? / Then let us meet them like necessities' (Pt 2, III. i. 92–3). As we would expect, there is nothing supernatural in his view of kingship. It is, for him, an office to be earned; his persistent habit of comparing Hal with Hotspur leads to one of his most characteristic utterances:

> Now by my sceptre, and my soul to boot,
> He hath more worthy interest to the state
> Than thou the shadow of succession.
> For of no right, nor colour like to right,
> He doth fill fields with harness in the realm.
>
> (Pt 1, III. ii. 97–101)

To reinforce this pragmatic view by swearing on his sceptre and his soul is another of Henry's unconscious ironies. In Part 2 we see what the crown means to him: a possession to be laid on his pillow, like a child's favourite toy. As York in *2 Henry VI* described himself as 'the silly owner of the goods' (I. i. 226) and thus destroyed the dignity of his claim, the language of Henry's rebuke to Hal for stealing the crown is that of a middle-class father whose son has broken into the cashbox: 'How quickly nature falls into revolt / When gold becomes her object! (Pt 2, IV. v. 65–6). Though he predicts that the orderly succession from father to son will settle the dynastic problem, he also warns Hal that he will have to work to keep his position: 'all my friends, which thou must make thy friends, / Have but their stings and teeth newly ta'en out' (Pt 2, IV. v. 204–5). (This is a sad revelation of what the word 'friend' means in politics.)

—Alexander Leggatt, *Shakespeare's Political Drama: The History Plays and the Roman Plays* (London: Routledge, 1988), pp. 78–81

[Ralph Berry (b. 1931) a professor of English at Florida State University, has written *The Art of John Webster* (1972) and *Shakespearean Structures* (1981). In this extract from *Shakespeare and Social Class* (1988), Berry contrasts the portrayal of social classes in *Henry IV, Part One* with that of *Richard II*.]

The land is no longer defined in terms of its (ailing) ruler. Instead, the sprawling, autonomous vitality of the people is everywhere. This is epic drama, and one can do worse than touch it first at the small scene with the Carriers in the Rochester inn-yard. Here are the realities of work, early starts, the insanitary habits of the English, things going wrong, fleas, damp provender, livestock to be cared for, the absence of the people who used to see that things worked, the bustle and exhilaration of the early morning. The passing of Robin Ostler is lamented, no doubt as a Homeric formula: "Poor fellow never joyed since the price of oats rose, it was the death of him" (2.1.11–12). The extraordinary sense of life as it is lived, outside the subjectivities of the main personages, is everywhere. We even know the breakfast order of the travelers who "call for eggs and butter." Can reality be more pointed than that?

The play cannot be seen simply as The Education of a Prince, or The Adventures of Jack Falstaff. The major characters grow out of the teeming life all around, who all sense this outside world of classes, types, and humanity at large. Simply to list occupations and functionaries takes a little space: burgomaster, underskinker, vintner, grandjuror, franklin, clerk, sheriff, chamberlain, hangman, drawer, weaver, factor, inn-keeper, auditor. Of this world of beings and types, Falstaff knows a great deal, and Hal picks up a great deal. The play traces Hal's learning curve.

Something of this comes out in the prologue to the tavern scene. Hal becomes a field worker specializing in language, a cultural anthropologist among a tribe virtually unknown to him. His visit to the cellar, at the invitation of the drawers, has impressed him. People are usually impressed by a tour of the cellar. Hal has encountered the drinking habits of the drawers—

"when you breathe in your watering they cry 'Hem!' and bid you play it off" and concludes that "I am so good a proficient in one quarter of an hour that I can drink with any tinker in his own language during my life" (2.4. 16–19). This might be an overestimate. Hal has fallen into the classic trap of the anthropologist, who contaminates the data by being there to record it. The Carriers, in the presence of nobody but each other, speak a far more vivid and resourceful language than the drawers in the presence of the Prince.

Still, they add to the Prince's experience. The prime virtue of Hal is that he is prepared to experiment with roles, while retaining his identity. This is superbly symbolized in the play scene with Falstaff, when Hal first takes on the role of the Prince, then of the King himself. That, of course, is the role that most expresses him: *"I'll play my father"* (2.4.419). But just as Hal has seemed an undergraduate learning drinking practices, he puts on years in the encounter with the Sheriff who interrupts the play world. It is a neat cameo of a police inquiry, in which the detective must enter a house of multiple repute and discreetly interrogate a highly placed individual. The dangerous tensions of the matter are scrupulously depicted: the Prince may not deal with the situation via a simple discharge of vehemence; the official does his duty, but may not press it too hard. Both men tread a fine line, as the Prince finds a formula that the Sheriff can accept:

> The man I do assure you is not here,
> For I myself at this time have employed him"
> [a pause, surely, for the following "And" is suggestive]
> And Sheriff, I will engage my word to thee,
> That I will by tomorrow dinnertime
> Send him to answer thee, or any man.   (2.4.494–98)

It is an astonishingly mature performance. The ambivalent position of the Prince of Wales is turned to dramatic advantage: Shakespeare shows a young man not yet invested in the authority that will be his, having to deal with all social classes from tinkers to the Lord Chief Justice. Con men, friends, offers, criticisms, traps, he has to surmount them all. It is an education, and Hal devours it.

Hotspur, evidently, is a different story. The point about Hotspur is not that he is stupid, but that he might just as well be. There's an archaism, a resistance to learning in his mentality that makes him functionally obsolete—not to mention, dead. Dramatically, Shakespeare has solved the problem of *Henry VI*: how does one make attractive and interesting a representative of the quarrelsome nobility that swamps the dramatis personae? He creates an enormously vital, likeable young man, hotheaded to a fault, who considers his resistance to all forms of challenge as the absolute imperative of identity. The class governs the individual. There is nothing in Hotspur of the wary adaptability of Hal, evidence of a species headed for survival and progress.

> —Ralph Berry, *Shakespeare and Social Class* (Atlantic Highlands, NJ: Humanities Press, 1988), pp. 77–79

BARBARA HODGDON ON FALSTAFF'S FEMININE CHARACTERISTICS

[Barbara Hodgdon (b. 1932) is a professor of English at Drake University and the author of a study of *Henry IV, Part Two* (1993). In this extract from *The End Crowns All* (1991), a book on Shakespeare's history plays, Hodgdon discusses the exclusion of women in *Henry IV, Part One,* with the result that Falstaff gains some feminine characteristics.]

Unlike Shakespeare's earlier histories, where conflict centers on genealogical descent in a struggle for the crown's rightful ownership, *1 Henry IV* positions the Percy-Northumberland rebellion against the state so that it serves Hal's mimetic rivalry with Hotspur as well as that between his authentic and counterfeit fathers, Henry IV and Falstaff. In this extremely limited gender economy, structured by a desire for the male other that takes the form of aggression, women are positioned at history's margins: unnecessary to prove or deny Hal's or Hotspur's legitimacy (as, for instance, in *King John*), they simply delay historical time. Only the rebel leaders—Hotspur and Lord Mortimer—have wives, whose presence functions primarily to separate public from private domains and, by proving their husbands' heterosexuality, deflects the homoerotic into the homosocial; says Hotspur, "This is no world / To play with mammets or to tilt with lips" (2.3.87–88), nor has he time to listen to the Welsh lady sing (3.1.234). In their resistance to the male chivalric project, Kate Percy and Glendower's daughter are kin to Falstaff, a more substantial image of feminine "misrule," who lies within the tavern space, together with thieves, swaggerers, a Hostess-landlady, and "gentlewomen" who, it is said, "live honestly by the prick of their needles" (*Henry V*, 2.1.31–32). Although within the Oedipal narrative, Falstaff figures as Hal's surrogate father, he is coded in feminine, maternal terms: his fat belly is the masculine counterpart of the pregnant woman; his Rabelaisian excesses of food and drink make him the Carnival antithesis to Henry IV's ascetic Lenten identity and his world of religious penance, bent as Henry IV is on expiating personal as well as national guilt with a crusade. It is Falstaff who accuses Hal of being the king's bastard son, and Hal, too, imagines him as female when, just before baiting Falstaff about his Gadshill cowardice and with Hotspur circulating in his mind and in his talk, he thinks himself into playing Percy and "that damned brawn" into "Dame Mortimer his wife" (2.4.104–5). That "play extempore" is then transformed into one where the roles of king and son become interchangeable, shared between Falstaff and Hal, and where women have no place: Falstaff's first "command" as "father-king" is "convey my tristful queen" (2.4.375).

But perhaps the most telling of Falstaff's multiform female guises of misrule is his association with Queen Elizabeth's virgin identity: "Let us be Diana's foresters, gentlemen of the shade, minions of the moon; and let men say we be men of good government, being governed as the sea is, by our noble and chaste mistress the moon" (1.2.23–27). Desiring to undertake something like Essex's role in the annual Accession Day Tourneys that celebrated Elizabeth's powerfully mythic, theatricalized presence, his fantasy of social order would steal and invert Essex's chivalric image—echoed in Hotspur's "easy leap / To pluck bright honor from the pale-faced moon"

(1.3.201–2)—in order to recode his own body. Chivalry's daytime, however, cannot admit an aging, corpulent "squire of the night's body," whose *2 Henry IV* counterpart, mentioned in passing, is Shallow's "bona roba," Jane Nightwork (3.2.188). Even Hal, "a truant to chivalry" and the "shadow" of his father's succession (5.1.94), must transform himself to look the part of a May lord, "Ris[ing] from the ground like feathered Mercury . . . / As if an angel dropped down from the clouds," in order to confront Hotspur, a "Mars in swaddling clothes," the "king of honor" (4.1.106–8; 3.2.112; 4.1.10). And although Sir John's body is also capable of metamorphosis, his transformations, and the codes he serves, work precisely to expose such glorious disguises.

> —Barbara Hodgdon, *The End Crowns All: Closure and Contradiction in Shakespeare's History* (Princeton: Princeton University Press, 1991), pp. 155–56

BERNARD J. PARIS ON KING HENRY, HAL, AND HOTSPUR

[Bernard J. Paris (b. 1931), a professor of English at the University of Florida, has written several books, including *Character and Conflict in Jane Austen's Novels* (1978), *Bargains with Fate: Psychological Crises and Conflicts in Shakespeare and His Plays* (1991), and *Character as a Subversive Force in Shakespeare* (1991), from which the following extract is taken. Here, Paris maintains that Shakespeare makes it clear in *Henry IV, Part One* that King Henry is wrong in his denigration of Hal and his vaunting of Hotspur.]

In *1 Henry IV,* Hal's detractors are King Henry and Hotspur. In the opening scene Henry envies Northumberland for having "A son who is the theme of honour's tongue," while "riot and dishonour stain the brow / Of my young Harry"; and he wishes that Hotspur were his son instead of Henry. When Hal returns to court, the King attacks him for his "inordinate and low desires," accuses him of "vassal fear" and "Base inclination," and compares him unfavorably to Hotspur, who "hath more worthy interest to the state / Than thou, the shadow of succession" (3.2). Hotspur refers to him contemptuously as the "madcap Prince of Wales" (4.1) whom he "would have poisoned with a pot of ale" were it not for the fact that "his father loves him not / And would be glad he met with some mischance" (1.3). The play as a whole moves toward the battle of Shrewsbury where Hal proves both his loyalty and prowess, defeats one of his detractors, converts the other, and demonstrates his worthiness of the throne.

From the beginning, however, Shakespeare is at pains to let us know that Henry is wrong in his judgment of Hal's character and of his worth in relation to Hotspur. Immediately after the King's complaints about Hal, we see Hal with Falstaff, who is proposing that thievery be countenanced and gallows removed when Hal becomes king. The issue, says ⟨C. L.⟩ Barber, is whether "the interregnum of a Lord of Misrule, delightful in its moment, might develop into the anarchic reign of a favorite dominating a dissolute king." When Hal responds to Falstaff's "Do not thou, when thou art king, hang a thief" by saying that Falstaff shall "have the hanging of thieves" (1.2), he is making it clear that he will not be a dissolute king. Unlike the Prince in *The Famous Victories of Henry the Fifth*, Hal is not himself a criminal. He refuses to participate in the Gadshill affair ("Who, I rob? I a thief? Not I, by my faith"), wavers a moment under pressure from Falstaff ("Well, then, once in my days I'll be a madcap"), then determines to "tarry at home" (1.2). He goes along only after Poins proposes that the two of them rob the thieves rather than the travelers, and he arranges to have the booty returned.

Shakespeare's presentation of Hal in the second scene of the play is a response to Harry's complaints in the first. He raises the question through Falstaff's speeches of whether Hal will be a lawless king and immediately provides us with evidence that he will not. In case we have missed the point, Hal's soliloquy should leave no doubt. What this speech tells us about Hal's character is a matter of considerable controversy, but it seems fairly clear that it is an important rhetorical device. It lets us know that Hal is aware of the deficiencies of his companions and means to remain with them for only a limited period of time, that he will "throw off" his "loose behaviour" when the right moment arrives, and that he will live up to the demands of his role and the values of his community. The soliloquy generates a great deal of dramatic irony, since it gives us more information about Hal than is possessed by the characters in the play and makes us aware of the inappropriateness of their expectations and anxieties. It creates expectations in the audience that are then fulfilled by the ensuing action, partially in part 1 and completely in part 2. The expectation is not for reformation, but for vindication. We know that Henry and Hotspur are wrong about Hal, and we await their acknowledgement of his worth. We know that his vindication will seem like a reformation to other people, but we also know that Hal will not change in any fundamental way. Rather, he will appear to be what he really is; he will display his virtues at last.

As the play progresses, Shakespeare employs other foreshadowing devices that contribute to the rhetoric of vindication. Hal assures Falstaff that he is not afraid of the approaching confrontation with Douglas and Percy (2.4); he lets Falstaff know, only half in jest, that he will banish him (2.4); he promises his father that he "shall hereafter . . . / Be more [him]self" (3.2); and he predicts his battlefield triumphs, which will win him all the glory Percy has accumulated and will wash away his shame. Since the action confirms all that Hal says, we are left with the impression that he can do whatever he wishes; he is not torn between virtue and vice, nobility and degeneracy, but is simply choosing when to display his true self. His vindication, both in this play and the next, is foreshadowed also by Vernon's praise, which, coming from an adversary, carries much weight: "England did never owe so sweet a hope, / So much misconstrued in his wantonness" (5.3). There is a similar speech by Warwick in part 2, in which he tells Henry that his son "but studies his companions," whom he will "cast off" in "the perfectness of time" (4.4). His "memory" of them will help to form his judgment, thus "turning past evils to advantages." Both of these speeches present Hal not as a dissolute young man who will reform, but as a noble young man who has been "misconstrued," and the audience knows that they are right before the action proves them to be so.

In *1 Henry IV*, the primary contrast is between Prince Hal and Hotspur, to whom the King twice compares his son, to Hal's great disadvantage. Part of Shakespeare's rhetoric of vindication is to develop the comparison dramatically in such a way as to show Hal to be the better man, and this from the start. The King is mistaken not only about Hal, but also about Hotspur, who does embody certain martial virtues in which Hal is, for the moment, deficient, but who also embodies the defects of those virtues, and who behaves self-destructively as a result. Whereas Shakespeare consistently justifies Hal, he consistently satirizes Hotspur, who lacks all balance and self-control.

—Bernard J. Paris, "Prince Hal," *Character as a Subversive Force in Shakespeare: The History and Roman Plays* (Rutherford, NJ: Fairleigh Dickinson University Press, 1991), pp. 74–76

Books by
William Shakespeare

Venus and Adonis. 1593.

The Rape of Lucrece. 1594.

Henry VI. 1594.

Titus Andronicus. 1594.

The Taming of the Shrew. 1594.

Romeo and Juliet. 1597.

Richard III. 1597.

Richard II. 1597.

Love's Labour's Lost. 1598.

Henry IV. 1598.

The Passionate Pilgrim. 1599.

A Midsummer Night's Dream. 1600.

The Merchant of Venice. 1600.

Much Ado About Nothing. 1600.

Henry V. 1600.

The Phoenix and the Turtle. 1601.

The Merry Wives of Windsor. 1602.

Hamlet. 1603.

King Lear. 1608.

Troilus and Cressida. 1609.

Sonnets. 1609.

Pericles. 1609.

Othello. 1622.

Mr. William Shakespeares Comedies, Histories & Tragedies. Ed. John Heminge and Henry Condell. 1623 (First Folio), 1632 (Second Folio), 1663 (Third Folio), 1685 (Fourth Folio).

Poems. 1640.

Works. Ed. Nicholas Rowe. 1709. 6 vols.

Works. Ed. Alexander Pope. 1723–25. 6 vols.

Works. Ed. Lewis Theobald. 1733. 7 vols.

Works. Ed. Thomas Hanmer. 1743–44. 6 vols.

Works. Ed. William Warburton. 1747. 8 vols.

Plays. Ed. Samuel Johnson. 1765. 8 vols.

Plays and Poems. Ed. Edmond Malone. 1790. 10 vols.

The Family Shakespeare. Ed. Thomas Bowdler. 1807. 4 vols.

Works. Ed. J. Payne Collier. 1842–44. 8 vols.

Works. Ed. H. N. Hudson. 1851–56. 11 vols.

Works. Ed. Alexander Dyce. 1857. 6 vols.

Works. Ed. Richard Grant White. 1857–66. 12 vols.

Works (Cambridge Edition). Ed. William George Clark, John Glover, and William Aldis Wright. 1863–66. 9 vols.

A New Variorum Edition of the Works of Shakespeare. Ed. H. H. Furness et al. 1871– .

Works. Ed. W. J. Rolfe. 1871–96. 40 vols.

The Pitt Press Shakespeare. Ed. A. W. Verity. 1890–1905. 13 vols.

The Warwick Shakespeare. 1893–1938. 13 vols.

The Temple Shakespeare. Ed. Israel Gollancz. 1894–97. 40 vols.

The Arden Shakespeare. Ed. W. J. Craig, R. H. Case et al. 1899–1924. 37 vols.

The Shakespeare Apocrypha. Ed. C. F. Tucker Brooke. 1908.

The Yale Shakespeare. Ed. Wilbur L. Cross, Tucker Brooke, and Willard Highley Durham. 1917–27. 40 vols.

The New Shakespeare (Cambridge Edition). Ed. Arthur Quiller-Couch and John Dover Wilson. 1921–62. 38 vols.

The New Temple Shakespeare. Ed. M. R. Ridley. 1934–36. 39 vols.

Works. Ed. George Lyman Kittredge. 1936.

The Penguin Shakespeare. Ed. G. B. Harrison. 1937–59. 36 vols.

The New Clarendon Shakespeare. Ed. R. E. C. Houghton. 1938– .

The Arden Shakespeare. Ed. Una Ellis-Fermor et al. 1951– .

The Complete Pelican Shakespeare. Ed. Alfred Harbage. 1969.

The Complete Signet Classic Shakespeare. Ed. Sylvan Barnet. 1972.

The Oxford Shakespeare. Ed. Stanley Wells. 1982– .

The New Cambridge Shakespeare. Ed. Philip Brockbank. 1984– .

Works about William Shakespeare and *Henry IV, Part One*

Baker, Christopher. "The Christian Context of Falstaff's 'Finer End.'" *Explorations in Renaissance Culture* 12 (1986): 68–86.

Bergeron, David M., ed. *Pageantry in the Shakespearean Theater*. Athens: University of Georgia Press, 1986.

Black, James. "'Anon, Anon, Sir': Discourse of Occasion in *Henry IV*." *Cahiers Elisabethains* 37 (1990): 27–42.

Blanpied, John. *Time and the Artist in Shakespeare's History Plays*. Newark: University of Delaware Press, 1983.

Bloom, Harold, ed. *Falstaff*. New York: Chelsea House, 1992.

———, ed. *William Shakespeare's* Henry IV, Part 1. New York: Chelsea House, 1987.

Booth, Stephen. "The Shakespearean Actor as Kamikaze Pilot." *Shakespeare Quarterly* 36 (1985): 553–70.

Calderwood, James. *Metadrama in Shakespeare's Henriad*. Berkeley: University of California Press, 1979.

Everett, Barbara. "The Fatness of Falstaff: Shakespeare and Character." *Proceedings of the British Academy* 76 (1990): 109–28.

Faber, M. D. "Falstaff Behind the Arras." *American Imago* 27 (1970): 197–225.

Fehrenbach, Robert J. "When Lord Cobham and Edmund Tilney 'Were at Odds': Oldcastle, Falstaff, and the Date of *1 Henry IV*." *Shakespeare Studies* 18 (1986): 87–101.

Gash, Anthony. "Shakespeare's Comedies of Shadow and Substance: Word and Image in *Henry IV* and *Twelfth Night*." *Word and Image* 4 (1988): 626–62.

Goldberg, Jonathan. "The Commodity of Names: 'Falstaff' and 'Oldcastle' in *1 Henry IV*." *Bucknell Review* 35, No. 2 (1992): 76–88.

Gottschalk, Paul. "Hal, and the 'Play Extempore' in *1 Henry IV*." *Texas Studies in Literature and Language* 15 (1974): 604–14.

Greenblatt, Stephen. "Invisible Bullets: Renaissance Authority and Its Subversion, *Henry IV* and *Henry V*." In *Political Shakespeare,* ed. Jonathan Dollimore and Alan Sinfield. Manchester, UK: Manchester University Press, 1985, pp. 18–47.

Hart, Jonathan. "Temporality and Theatricality in Shakespeare's Lancastrian Tetralogy." *Studia Neophilologica* 63 (1991): 69–88.

Hawkins, Sherman. "*Henry IV:* The Structural Problem Revisited." *Shakespeare Quarterly* 33 (1982): 278–301.

Highley, Christopher. "Wales, Ireland, and *Henry IV*." *Renaissance Drama* 21 (1990): 91–114.

Hillman, Richard. " 'Not Amurath an Amurath Succeeds': Playing Doubles in Shakespeare's Henriad." *English Literary Renaissance* 21 (1991): 161–89.

Hunt, Maurice. "Time and Timelessness in *1 Henry IV*." *Explorations in Renaissance Culture* 10 (1984): 56–66.

Jones, Robert C. *These Valiant Dead: Renewing the Past in Shakespeare's Histories.* Iowa City: University of Iowa Press, 1991.

Kerrigan, John. "*Henry IV* and the Death of Old Double." *Essays in Criticism* 40 (1990): 24–53.

MacLean, Hugh. " 'Looking Before and After': Hal and Hamlet Once More." *Papers on Language and Literature* 23 (1987): 273–89.

Manheim, Michael. *The Weak King Dilemma in the Shakespearean History Play.* Syracuse, NY: Syracuse University Press, 1973.

Pierce, Robert B. *Shakespeare's History Plays: The Family and the State.* Columbus: Ohio State University Press, 1971.

Prior, Moody E. *The Drama of Power: Studies in Shakespeare's History Plays.* Evanston, IL: Northwestern University Press, 1973.

Racklin, Phyllis. *Stages of History: Shakespeare's English Chronicles.* Ithaca, NY: Cornell University Press, 1990.

Ribner, Irving. *The English History Play in the Age of Shakespeare.* Princeton: Princeton University Press, 1957.

Scoufos, Alice-Lyle. *Shakespeare's Typological Satire: A Study of the Falstaff-Oldcastle Problem.* Athens: Ohio University Press, 1979.

Smidt, Kristian. *Unconformities in Shakespeare's History Plays.* London: Macmillan, 1982.

Thayer, C. G. *Shakespearean Politics: Government and Misgovernment in the Great Histories.* Athens: Ohio University Press, 1983.

Tillyard, E. M. W. *Shakespeare's History Plays.* London: Chatto & Windus, 1944.

Traub, Valerie. "Prince Hal's Falstaff: Positioning Psychoanalysis and the Female Reproductive Body." *Shakespeare Quarterly* 40 (1989): 456–74.

Traversi, Derek A. *Shakespeare from* Richard II *to* Henry IV. Stanford: Stanford University Press, 1957.

Watson, Donald G. *Shakespeare's Early History Plays: Politics at Play on the Elizabethan Stage.* Athens: University of Georgia Press, 1990.

West, Gillian. "Falstaff's Punning." *English Studies* 69 (1988): 541–58.

———. "Hardyng's Chronicle and Shakespeare's Hotspur." *Shakespeare Quarterly* 41 (1990): 348–51.

Wilders, John. *The Lost Garden.* London: Macmillan, 1978.

Willems, Michele. "Misconstruction in *1 Henry IV.*" *Cahiers Elisabethains* 37 (1990): 43–57.

Wilson, J. Dover. *The Fortunes of Falstaff.* New York: Macmillan, 1944.

Index of
Themes and Ideas

47, 49–50, 53, 63–65, 68, 70–71, 74, 76–79; Hotspur killed by, 21-22, 24; Hotspur praised by, 19–20; king's denigration of, 13, 17, 47–50, 58–60, 70–71, 76–79; legitimacy of, 48–50, 74, 75; political shrewdness of, 15, 20, 23, 43; princely role accepted by, 21, 22, 40–42, 76–79; reform promised by, 13–14, 15, 16, 17, 23, 41–42, 45, 77–78

HENRY IV: artificial identity of, 59–60, 69–70; crusade planned by, 13, 33–34, 38, 41, 46–47, 75; and death of Richard II, 13, 19, 22, 35; Falstaff as foil to, 17–18, 48, 60–63; guilt of, 58–60; Hal denigrated by, 13, 17, 47–50, 58–60, 70–71, 76–79; as hypocrite, 35, 38; malaise suffered by, 70–71; moral blindness of, 48; Richard II compared to, 34–35, 38–39, 47–48, 70–71, Richard III compared to, 71

HENRY IV, PART ONE: class distinctions in, 63–65, 72–74; deception in, 67–71; dramatic balance in, 52–53; English social life in, 16, 52, 72–74; exclusion of women in, 74–76; historical basis of, 56–58; misinformation in, 69; political intrigues in, 33–35, 46–48, 50–52; prose in, 6, 13; structure of, 50–53; time in, 5, 6, 40–42

HENRY IV, PART TWO, and how it compares, 66, 69, 71, 76, 78

HENRY V, and how it compares, 6, 22, 66

MERRY WIVES OF WINDSOR, THE, and how it compares, 5

MORTIMER, and his role in the play, 14–15, 16, 19, 24, 34–35, 38, 51, 68

NORTHUMBERLAND, and his role in the play, 13, 14–15, 18, 22, 24, 51, 68, 69, 70

ORDER VS. DISORDER, as theme, 18, 22, 23, 33–35, 37–39, 48, 60–63

PERCY, HENRY ("HOTSPUR"): and chivalric code, 14, 18, 20, 22, 23–24, 43–45, 63–65, 74; Glendower disliked by, 51–52; Hal compared to, 13, 14, 17, 20, 22, 23, 43–45, 47, 49–50, 53, 63–65, 68, 70–71, 74, 76–79; as heir-apparent, 49–50, 74; impatience of, 14–15, 16–17, 21, 44–45, 78; redemption theme and, 42